I0488000

Offshore Basics
Features of A Special Business Area

by
Levent Gülkök

Writers Club Press
San Jose New York Lincoln Shanghai

Offshore Basics
Features of A Special Business Area

Copyright © 2000 by Levent Gülkök

This book may not be reproduced or distributed, in whole
or in part, in print or by any other means without the written
permission of the author.

ISBN: 0-595-09154-7

Published by Writers Club Press, an imprint of iUniverse.com, Inc.

For information address:
iUniverse.com, Inc.
620 North 48th Street
Suite 201
Lincoln, NE 68504-3467
www.iuniverse.com

URL: http://www.writersclub.com

Dedicated to
my family with gratitude for their patience, support and love.

Contents

Foreword

The purpose of this book is to give an overview about the most important features of offshore business. Additionally, it is the intention of the author to describe the most used offshore jurisdictions with their typical characteristics. Most chapters in this book are written with reference to United Kingdom companies and companies incorporated in offshore jurisdictions, which generally follow UK Company law.

Introduction

The historical and the continuing primary attraction of incorporation is to limit the liability of investors. Limited liability legislation was first introduced in the nineteenth century and allowed companies to be set up which limited the loss to the owners to the amount of the share capital which the owners had paid for or undertaken to pay for. This type of legislation was promulgated to encourage business investment and enterprise. Previously an investor might have faced complete and utter ruin in the event of the failure of his business because he would remain personally liable for all the debts of that business.

Liability was limited by virtue of the principle that the company was a distinct legal person from its proprietor so that creditors were only able to look to the assets of the company for payment rather than the assets of the person who might have invested in that company.

Because a company is a legal entity distinct from its shareholders and directors, profits received by a company will generally be taxed at the rate to which the company is subject rather than at the rate to which the shareholders are subject in their country of residence. Thus a resident of a high tax country can set up a company which is subject to a rate of tax which is low or zero and may arrange for profits to be booked into the name of that company thereby making a saving equal to the difference between the corporate rate of tax and the shareholders personal tax rate. The shareholder can be subject to anti-avoidance legislation in his country of residence which may impact on the effectiveness of these arrangements but creative and skillful structuring can make that anti-avoidance legislation inapplicable.

If the company make payments then those payments would normally be taxable in the hands of the recipient so the greatest advantage is achieved by letting the profits roll up within the company account so that tax is deferred indefinitely or avoided completely. If profits can remain untaxed offshore then not only is tax saved on the original profit but also on the investment income generated by reinvesting those profits so the benefit is cumulative and substantive.

The offshore islands off the coast of Europe and North America were the classic offshore financial centers. They were characterized by low taxes or no taxes, compliance requirements which were rather less than in the more populated countries and they might also have had flourishing finance sectors dealing with the monies which they received from neighboring high tax countries. If this describes the original sense of the word offshore the word is now defined by its extended characteristics so that landlocked countries such as Luxembourg, Monaco and Andorra are also now generally referred to as being offshore financial center.

People sometimes ask which is the best offshore area in which to incorporate. There can be no standard reply as the answer really depends upon the intended use of the corporation and upon the business circumstances. There are, however, a number of factors, which must be considered. The first is the tax regime on the offshore financial center and just as important is the political and economic stability. The offshore financial center chosen should not be subject to violent political swings or the likelihood of military coup or invasion. Other factors include the quality of communications, language, legal system, confidentiality, exchange controls and banking facilities. Attention should also be given to restrictions, which the country might impose upon certain types of business. An obvious factor is cost like registration fees, flat rate taxes, incorporation fees, domiciliary and management fees. Of particular importance is to remind that the tax and the other benefits which can be obtained will depend not only upon the tax and other legislation of the country of residence, and possibly the domicile, of the beneficial owner but also any relevant anti-avoidance legislation of any country in which someone intends to do business. It is always to encourage everyone to take appropriate independent professional advice before setting up an offshore structure.

I
Features of Taxation

1. 1. Tax Residency

It is a common misconception that both a company and an individual may only be tax resident in one jurisdiction at any one time. Most countries will tax an individual who spends six months within their borders. Thus, by way of simple example an individual who spends six months in the United Kingdom and the other six months in the USA may be considered as tax resident in both the US and the UK and subject to tax on his worldwide income in both countries. Happily, the US and UK have signed a double taxation but the individual would be subject to the highest level of taxation applicable in either country.

A similar position can arise in respect of companies. Most countries consider any company that is incorporated within their jurisdiction to be tax resident but also consider any company which is managed and controlled within their jurisdiction to be tax resident. A Company is generally considered to be managed and controlled wherever its directors habitually meet and reside. Thus, a similar position to that of the unfortunate individual mentioned above can be reached where a US incorporated company has a board of directors who meet and reside in the United Kingdom. The US would seek to tax the company on its worldwide income because the company was incorporated within the US and the UK Inland Revenue would seek to tax that same company on its worldwide income because it is managed and controlled from within the United Kingdom. By the same token any offshore company managed and controlled from the United Kingdom would be subject to UK tax on its worldwide income. Because of this management and control test it will rarely be the case that someone residing onshore can safely act as the director of an offshore company without making that company liable to tax in his home jurisdiction.

1.2. Exempt Companies

Many offshore areas have initiated exempt company legislation which means that companies beneficially owned by non resident individuals which have no income arising in the jurisdiction of incorporation may be managed and controlled from the jurisdiction without tax consequence. For example Gibraltar allows a company to be structured so as to be Gibraltar resident but as long as that company is owned by non residents of Gibraltar and does not do any business with Gibraltar resident companies or individuals then the company may apply to be exempted from Gibraltar tax.

1. 3. Non Resident Versus No Tax

Some areas only give non-tax status to non-resident companies i.e. companies incorporated in the jurisdiction but managed and controlled elsewhere. Other offshore areas do not levy corporation tax irrespective of ownership or structure. Bahamas, Cayman and the Turks & Caicos Islands are all major no tax jurisdiction which do not impose tax on individuals or companies which are either incorporated or managed and controlled within their jurisdiction. For this reason a non-resident company could also be controlled from any of those jurisdiction with impunity. From the foregoing it can be seen that correctly structuring and administering the company is of paramount importance to its taxability.

II
Legal Framework

2. 1. Company Name

The former of a company is required to nominate a suitable name as the Registrar has the power to refuse registration of any name, which he considers undesirable. The Registrar will also refuse a name if it is too like that of an existing company. In the United Kingdom, refusal on this ground is limited to a name, which is identical with an existing name. It is, of course, the responsibility of the former to choose a name, which does not cause confusion with an existing name. In many jurisdictions a name will not be permitted if it suggests that a company with small resources is trading on a great scale or over a wide field. Certain words may be regarded as being sensitive such as trust, investment, bank, insurance and can only be used if the company is specifically licensed to undertake the indicated activity.

There are however, variations in treatment between jurisdictions; the words international and trust are freely allowed in the Republic of Ireland but in the Isle of Man use of the word international would have to be justified by the company having a paid-in capital of at least £ 100. 000.

2.2. Authorized and Issued Share Capital

The amount of the authorized capital, that is the capital available to be issued, can be as high as the investor chooses. The issued share capital, the capital actually taken up by shareholders, may be paid, partly paid or issued for a consideration other than cash. Once shares have been wholly paid for then the shareholder has no further liability to the company. If the shareholder does not pay for his shares or pays only in part then he can be called upon to pay the balance outstanding at any time and would always be subject to a call if the company cannot otherwise pay its debts.

In most jurisdictions capitalization taxes are levied in respect of the amount of the authorized share capital so generally a company would be incorporated with the highest authorized share capital for which the minimum amount of registration fees apply. If shares are to be held by nominee or trustee shareholders such shares would normally be fully paid up so as to avoid liability for the professional shareholders.

2.3. Domiciliary Requirements

All companies must have a registered office within the country of incorporation at which process may be served and official notices received. However, this does not have to be the place where the actual business is carried on nor do the books of account necessarily have to be kept at the registered office.

Companies incorporated in many jurisdictions can have additional domiciliary requirements such as a requirement to maintain a resident agent or local resident representative who would be the person upon whom process would be served or to whom official notices would be sent. Some offshore jurisdictions also require companies to have a locally resident company secretary or director.

It is usually the responsibility of the company secretary to make sure that a company is in good standing and makes the necessary returns to the Registrar and Government. This requires a thorough knowledge of local company law and practice so it is strongly recommended that a locally based professional company secretary is appointed even though there may be no strict legal requirement to do so.

In some jurisdictions the office of company secretary is non-statutorily recognized so there is no legal requirement to appoint a company secretary. However, it will almost always be the case that it is a practical requirement to appoint a company secretary as banks and other third parties will not accept documentation unless it is signed by the company secretary.

2.4. Memorandum and Articles of Association

The objects of the company will be set out in the Memorandum of Association and the company is not legally capable of doing anything which is not authorized by its memorandum so normal practice is to draft extremely wide powers for a company with care being taken to ensure that all the proposed and future activities of the company are fully set out. In a number of jurisdictions, however, such as the Isle of Man, Liberia, Panama, Turks & Caicos Islands (for Exempted Companies), and the British Virgin Islands (for International Business Companies), no ultra vireos rule applies. Companies incorporated in those jurisdictions therefore may undertake any lawful business, which is not specifically proscribed or licensable. Thus the memorandum of companies incorporated in these jurisdictions may simply state that the objects are unlimited rather than exhaustively listing those objects.

The Memorandum of Association sets out the reason for which the company is to be formed and gives details of those who subscribe to the company but the Articles of Association represent a contract between the shareholders and the company. They provide detailed rules for the management of the company's affairs and for the conduct of its business. In some jurisdictions the Articles are referred to as "Bye-Laws".

2.5. Shareholders, Directors and Secretaries

Shareholders are the legal owners of the company. A United Kingdom private company may now only have one shareholder – previously such a company required at least two shareholders. Under the Articles of Association responsibility for the management of the company rests with its directors and to a limited extend with the company secretary. The shareholder would normally retain the power to remove a director from office and elect a replacement but should not interfere with the management of the company and do not have power to do so. In the case of a small UK company set up for the purpose of doing business in Britain it is quite common for the shareholders to double up as the directors and secretary of the company.

In offshore jurisdictions there may be variations in the minimum number of shareholders. In the Turks & Caicos Islands a company may have only one shareholder whereas in Hong Kong the minimum number is two.

In jurisdictions, which require a public record of the details of the shareholders to be maintained the shareholders of record will frequently be nominees, or trustees who will hold the shares for the beneficial owner thereby allowing anonymity to be retained.

As already mentioned earlier, professional third party directors who reside and meet in a fiscally neutral overseas jurisdiction would normally be employed so as to prevent the company being considered as resident in the high tax country where the owners reside or elsewhere.

Mention is commonly made of "nominee directors" this being reference to the idea that the directors of a company will carry out the instructions of the ultimate owner of the company. It is better to use the expression "third party directors" who might follow the suggestions of the ultimate owner. It is important that the directors do not blindly follow directions from any third party as otherwise it is clear that the control and management rests with the instructing party and not with the directors. Under these circumstances the company would then be considered as tax resident wherever the instructing party resides. Thus if the tax status of the company is not to be prejudiced it should be capable of demonstration that the directors do, in fact, manage and control the company and are not the puppets of a third party. The directors would normally look to the beneficial owner for guidance and would follow his whishes regarding the affairs of the company unless there was some overriding legal or other reason as to why those suggestions are inappropriate but the directors should consider those whishes carefully and independently.

2.6. Registered Shares Versus Bearer Shares

In some jurisdictions companies may issue shares in either registered or bearer form. Shares issued in registered form must be transferred by written instrument and the shareholder holds a certificate upon which their name appears. Bearer shares are transferred by delivery and the shareholder holds a certificate, which states simply that "the bearer" owns the shares in question. The holder of bearer shares undoubtedly enjoys greater confidentiality and can transfer his shares with greater ease but he also enjoys less security. If a bearer share certificate is lost or stolen then whoever next has physical possession of the share certificate becomes the shareholder and the owner of the company. The previous holder of the shares has little or no redress. Registered shares carry no such security risk and are still able to offer a high degree of confidentiality as in many jurisdictions the details of registered shareholders are not publicly registered. In jurisdictions which require public reporting anonymity can be retained by the use of nominee shareholders. Thus, because of the greater security afforded by registered shares and the fact that there is no real loss of confidentiality it is generally recommend that shares be issued in registered rather than bearer form.

III
Typical Uses and Examples of Offshore Companies

3.1. Trading Companies

An importing or exporting company might establish itself in an offshore area. The offshore company would take orders directly from the customer, but have the goods delivered directly to that customer from the manufacturer or place of purchase. The profits arising out of the difference between purchase price and sales price would then be accumulated in either a tax free or low tax area. With such trading companies, it is important to choose an offshore area, which has good communications, as shipping and other documentation may be critical to the scheme.

3.2. Investment Companies

Funds accumulated through investment companies set up in offshore areas can be invested or deposited throughout the world and whilst generally returns or interest payable in respect of these funds will be subject to local taxation, there are a number of offshore areas in which funds may be placed either in tax free bonds or as bank deposits where interest is paid gross. Similarly, in many offshore areas no capital gains taxes are applicable. Use of an offshore company incorporated in a suitable country allows the possibility of investing tax efficiently in a high tax country where there is a concessionaire tax treaty in respect of investments made by companies incorporated in the offshore country.

3.3. Holding Companies

Use may be made of an offshore holding company, which would fund the operation of subsidiaries in various countries so that the subsidiaries obtain the benefit of tax deductions on interest paid. If the holding company is situated in an offshore area where there are no income or corporation taxes and no requirement that dividends must be paid, then the profits which are accumulated in the tax free climate can be used to fund the requirement of subsidiaries or reinvested as business convenience suggests.

3.4. Probate and Privacy

A high net worth individual with properties or other assets in a number of countries may wish to hold these through the medium of a personal holding company so that upon his demise probate would be applied for in the country in which his company was incorporated rather than in each of the countries in which he might hold assets. This saves legal fees and avoids publicity. Again, not everybody wishes to advertise wealth and an individual may wish to hold property through an offshore entity simply because of the privacy, which the offshore arrangement gives.

3.5. Property Owning Companies

There are often great advantages in using an offshore property holding company for the purpose of holding an overseas property. Advantages of offshore property ownership include avoidance of inheritance tax, avoidance of capital gains tax, ease of sale which is achieved by transferring the shares in the company rather than transferring the property owned by the company and reduction of property purchase costs to the onward purchasers. Taking the example of investment in property in the United Kingdom by an offshore company, use of an appropriate off-shore vehicle can offer relief from income tax, capital gains tax and inheritance tax. It should be remembered, in particular, that when a non-resident company disposes of a property investment, no capital gains tax is charged and holding through an offshore company removes the application of inheritance tax which would apply if a non-domiciled investor held a UK property in his personal name.

3.6. Professional Services

Individuals, who receive substantial fees in respect of their professional services in capacities such as designers, consultants, authors or entertainers, may assign or contract with an offshore company the right to receive those fees. The Offshore-Employment-Company may not have to pay tax on its profits, which can be reinvested in a tax-free climate to generate further income from the offshore company. Payments to the individuals concerned can be structured in such a way as to minimize their tax liabilities. One example in this regard in respect of an overseas employment is to increase subsistence expenses as against fees as such, which would be paid to the individual.

3.7. Shipping Companies

The use of offshore shipping companies can eliminate direct or indirect taxation on shipping. Shipping companies may own or charter ships, the profits from which activities can be accumulated tax-free. Tax and legal requirements generally dictate that the offshore company owning a shipping vessel should be incorporated in the jurisdiction whose flag the ship flies. The historic havens for these purposes have been Panama and Liberia. Latterly, the registries of other nations have expanded and consideration might be given to registrations at British Ports of Registry such as those in the Isle of Man and Gibraltar. A certain prestige attaches to the registration of a ship or indeed a yacht at a British port of registry and the vessel can be surveyed at most ports throughout the world by a surveyor recognized by the UK Department of Trade and Industry. The British flag has always been regarded, as one of the worlds most dependable.

3.8. Patent, Copyright and Royalty Companies

An offshore company can purchase or be assigned the right to use a copyright, patent, trademark or know-how by its original holders with a power to sublicense. Upon acquisition of the intellectual property right the offshore company can then enter into agreement with licensees around the world who would be able to exploit the intellectual property right in various countries. It is thought preferable to acquire, for example, a patent at the patent pending stage before it becomes very valuable so that the capital payment for the acquisition of the patent can be set at a lower amount. Often royalties paid out of a high tax area attract withholding taxes at source. In many cases an interposing holding company may allow a reduction in the rate of tax withheld at source.

3.9. Insurance Companies

There are a number of offshore havens which are keen to encourage the establishment of insurance companies which like banking companies bring employment and investment to the country of incorporation and generally enhance its reputation and its range of financial services. In a number of offshore havens it is possible to incorporate insurance companies which pay no tax in respect of their premium or investment income.

3.10. Captive Insurance

Captive insurance companies have been created by many multinational companies to insure and re-insure the risks of subsidiaries and affiliated companies. Captive insurance companies are particularly suitable for the shipping and petroleum industries and for the insurance of risks, which might be insurable only at prohibitive premiums.

Bermuda and Guernsey have long been favored as domiciles for the incorporation of captive insurance companies with countries such as the Isle of Man and the Turks & Caicos Islands competing for a share of this growing market.

3.11. Banking Companies

Many offshore banking institutions have been established in tax havens in recent years. Many of these institutions are subsidiaries of major international banks. Such institutions pay interest free of withholding tax and engage in international financing from offshore bases, which are free from exchange controls. Such banking institutions and their associated trust companies are able to provide a wide range of financial services to their international clientele. Offshore banking institutions are also used by the smaller business Organization and indeed in some cases by individual owners to act as offshore cash management centers.

In the past, certain offshore centers such as Montserrat and Anguilla have lacked the supervision, which should accompany the setting up of smaller banking institutions. Indeed the British Government introduced a moratorium on the setting up of banking institutions in its Caribbean dependencies until such time as adequate legislation had been brought in and bank supervisors appointed. Of these jurisdictions one of the first to meet British Government requirements was the Turks and Caicos Islands. Under its banking regime two types of license are available, namely, a national and an overseas, the latter only permitting banking activities outside the Islands. In either case a bank would have to maintain a physical or representative presence in the Islands. A combined license can be granted. The management of the proposed bank would be required to display a sound knowledge of banking with evidence of ability and experience and no less than two directors must be appointed. In respect of those banks wishing to deal with the general public without restriction, substantial capital resources would have to be demonstrated. One jurisdiction which does permit the setting up of the smaller banking institutions, whilst at the same time providing a supervisory regime, is the Republic of Vanuatu (formerly known as the New Hebrides). Another Pacific jurisdiction favored by smaller institutions is Samoa.

IV
Banking Licenses

Obviously all jurisdictions, both onshore and offshore, have the facility to grant banking licenses to qualified applicants. In general terms, the onshore jurisdictions impose much stricter requirements on applicants and consequently the cost of setting up a bank in those jurisdictions would be greatly increased. The offshore jurisdictions offer some interesting possibilities because:

- They will allow a bank to operate free of tax on profit and
- It is possible to set up a bank without the need to maintain a physical presence within the jurisdiction other than that, which can readily be provided by a service company.

The following looks at a cross-section of the available possibilities and procedures.

4.1. United Kingdom

Generally it is possible to make applications to the Bank of England to set up a bank in the United Kingdom. Amongst other requirements it is necessary to set up an actual office in the United Kingdom staffed by two responsible executive officers. These officers must necessarily have a detailed knowledge of banking procedures and have therefore to expect to be paid salaries of between 35,000 and 70,000 Pounds Sterling. Suitable office space should have to be located, administrative support staff would have to be hired and computer systems should have to be installed which are sufficiently sophisticated to run all facets of a normal banking operation. The minimum required capital of an UK bank is 5 million ECU, all of which should have to be paid in and maintained as unimpaired reserves.

The United Kingdom is typical of many of the onshore jurisdictions and similar standards would apply in all other European Union countries as standard criteria have been adopted under the applicable European Union directives on banking. It is difficult to estimate the costs of setting up a bank in the United Kingdom but it would be unlikely that these would be less than US$ 220,000 and, as described, substantial annual running costs would necessarily be incurred. Additionally, the worldwide profits of the bank would be taxable at the normal UK rate of 33%. Similar costs and procedures would be experienced in the USA, Canada and other mainstream onshore jurisdictions.

4.2. Gibraltar

Gibraltar is a full member of the European Union so similar requirements are imposed on banks incorporated in Gibraltar as those noted above for UK banks. However, Gibraltar has certain distinct advantages:

a) Banks can obtain exempt status and therefore operate completely free of tax;

b) The costs of office space and staff are considerably lower in Gibraltar;

c) There are currently no banking applications pending in Gibraltar so the time-scale between the application for and granting of a banking license can be considerably reduced;

d) Again, the majority of the costs would be incurred in having to employ two executive directors/managers with the requisite experience and in installing the computers and systems, which are appropriate for a banking institution.

4.3. The British West Indies

In the 1970s and 1980s many of the British Dependent Territories were happy to accept applications for banking licenses with a minimum of paperwork and fuss. Some time ago the United Kingdom imposed increased standards on these territories so they are now unwilling to receive applications from anybody other than existing international recognized banks.

4.4. Antigua

Antigua is an independent Caribbean Island which is currently welcoming applications for a banking license which are unrestricted (expect from a prohibition on doing business with residents of the Caricom area). There is a requirement to have a paid in capital of US$ 1 million but no requirements regarding capital reserves or loan ratios are imposed and no physical presence on the island is needed which cannot be provided by a management company. Antigua therefore represents a real possibility to obtain an unrestricted license without the considerable costs, which would be experienced in most other competitive jurisdictions. The capital requirement is higher than that which is experienced in some of the Pacific Rim Islands but Antigua is one of the few places where an unrestricted license is available with relative ease.

4.5. Nauru

Nauru offers the possibility of setting up a bank with no requirement for local directors or any local presence apart from a registered office and company secretary in Nauru. Nauru accepts applications for unrestricted licenses or for in-house type banks but in practice the authorities are unwilling to grant unrestricted licenses to anybody other than an existing bank and would also impose a requirement that the applicant set up an office and associated infrastructure in Nauru. The capital requirements for an in-house bank are low – US$ 100,000. A Nauru in-house bank is prohibited from dealing with anybody other than associated companies and individuals but it is possible for the applicant to set up a finance company, which conducted a broader range of activities. For example, the finance company could take deposits from third parties and would then deposit the money with the bank. Any literature, which was drafted, could make clear reference to the fact that the finance company was a wholly owned subsidiary of XYZ Bank Ltd. and contain further detail about the bank.

4.6. Vanuatu

This is another jurisdiction, which has indicated it is willing to receive applications for both unrestricted and restricted licenses. The minimum criteria laid down is that each type of bank requires a paid in capital of US$ 150,000 but in practice it is unlikely that an unrestricted license could be obtained by offering this minimum required level of capitalization.

4.7. Samoa

Samoa is one of the offshore jurisdictions, which currently offer restricted offshore banking licenses. Unrestricted licenses are not obtainable by anybody other than existing banks and require a minimum paid up capital of US$ 10 million. This will probably be unattractive to most applicants. Restricted licenses require a minimum paid up capital of US$ 250,000 but the operations of the bank must be run through a local trust company. This does mean that an element of third party control and involvement in the affairs of the bank is required.

4.8. Bahamas

The Bahamas are an independent member of the British Commonwealth and a major financial center in their own right. The Bahamas welcomes applications for both unrestricted and restricted banking licenses. The minimum capitalization for an unrestricted license is US$ 1 million. This type of license can be obtained by private individuals but only if they are able to show that they have substantial high net worth. Restricted licenses are more readily granted to financial institutions. A restricted license enables the holder to provide banking and/or trust services only to a specified class of associated individuals or companies who would normally be named in the license or in a schedule attached to the license. The minimum paid up capital is only US$ 100,000. Both types of banks must maintain reserves in cash, or near cash, equal to 20-25% of deposits.

4.9. Some Additional Requirements

1. References from a leading bank, leading firm of lawyers and leading firm of accountants on each shareholder and each director.
2. Police clearances.
3. Evidence to satisfy the authorities that the shareholders/promoter(s) of the bank have substantial wealth and assets.
4. A detailed business plan which outlines the type of business that the bank will undertake, the way in which that business will be handled by the bank and estimates of turnover for the first 3 years. This is perhaps the most important document.
5. Evidence that the required minimum capital is available.
6. Curriculum Vitae on all directors and shareholders which should show some expertise in running a financial institution / bank.

This is the minimum required documentation. The list is not necessarily exhaustive. As can be seen, some authorities will require that local directors be employed who are actually going to run the bank. In all jurisdictions it is always helpful if a local director who has banking expertise attaches his name to the application especially if the other directors are unable to show any relevant experience. Ultimately the choice of jurisdiction will depend largely on what business the investor wish to undertake in the name of the bank and whether or not he wishes to set up a physical presence in the jurisdiction of incorporation.

V
Features of Trusts

5.1. Introduction

Many people prefer not to think about what will happen on their death but none of us are immortal and failure to make proper plans can mean that we leave behind a mess which has to be sorted out by our nearest and dearest at great expense and inconvenience at a time when they are emotionally vulnerable. Many individuals seek to put order to their affairs by making a comprehensive will. Under this arrangement the Executors named in the will would apply for a grant of probate, take possession of the assets of the deceased and then distribute those assets according to the terms of the will. These arrangements are perfectly in order but result in high administration costs (often around 4% of the total value of the estate), long time delays (even a simple estate would normally take at least one year to be wound up) and will often mean that considerable sums become payable in inheritance tax or estate duty. One alternative to a will arrangement is to set up a trust structure during lifetime which, with careful planning, can operate to eradicate these delays, administration costs and taxes as well as giving a large number of additional benefits. For these reasons the use of trusts is increasing dramatically.

5.2. Trust Concept

The concept of a trust was first used in Anglo Saxon times and is an arrangement whereby property is transferred from one person (the settlor) to another person or corporate body (the trustee) to hold the property for the benefit of a specified list or class of persons (the beneficiaries). Although a trust can be created solely by verbal agreement it is normal for a written document to be prepared which evidences the creation of the trust (the Trust Deed), sets out the terms and conditions upon which the trust assets are held by the Trustees and outlines the rights of the Beneficiaries. In essence, a trust is not dissimilar to a will except those assets are transferred to trustees during lifetime rather than those assets being transferred to executors on death. The trust deed is analogous to the deed of will.

Those unfamiliar with the trust concept usually express concern at the idea of transferring ownership of their property to a trustee. However, this concern can be alleviated if the trust concept and the distinction between legal ownership as contrasted with beneficial ownership is properly understood and the trust is governed by a sound trust law which can be enforced in a reputable jurisdiction.

The distinction between legal and beneficial ownership in English law evolved over centuries and has been transferred to many jurisdictions around the world, either through the adoption of English common law and equitable principles or as part of the express legislation of local law. International recognition of trusts has also been achieved by The Hague Trusts Convention, which has been signed, ratified and implemented by a number of countries.

5.3. Legal and Beneficial Ownership

The practical advantages of a trust are derived from the fact that a distinction is drawn between the formal or "legal" owner of property and the person who in reality has the use or benefit of the property - the "beneficial" owner. Thus for formal legal purposes the trustee is recognized as the owner whereas the person who has the use or benefit of the property (the beneficiaries) are protected by a body of legal rules which impose very strict duties on trustees and the way in which they administer the trust property. It is possible for the settlor to retain an interest in the trust and, for example, to be an actual or potential beneficiary. However, in many jurisdictions this can have estate duty and tax disadvantages. Where the settlor retains an interest directly or indirectly in trust property it is important that the trustees remain independent and exercise proper control over the trust property. If the person who sets up the trust continues to exercise control over the trust assets this may render the trust void.

5.4. Accountability of Trustee

The law imposes strict obligations and rules on trustees including a duty to account for any benefits the trustee may have gained directly or indirectly from a trust. This goes beyond fraudulent abuse of position by a trustee. There is a basic rule that a trustee may not derive any advantage directly or indirectly from a trust unless expressly permitted by the trust, for example, where he is a professional trustee and the trust provides specifically for a right to make reasonable charges for services. However, full disclosure of the basis and amount of charges is required. Accordingly a professional trustee who derives some other indirect commercial advantage which is not fully disclosed and approved will be acting in breach of trust. This appears to be something which some institutional trustees forming part of larger commercial groups sometimes overlook where, for example, a trustee company arranges for trust investments to be handled by a fund management company within the same group and fees are charged for this service without authority in the trust document. Independent trust companies who do not give investment advice, on the other hand, are able to place money for investment without favor and switch from one investment adviser to another as performance or circumstances dictate whereas it is rare for the larger institution to use anybody other than their own associated companies for investment irrespective of performance

5.5. Duty of Trustee to Obey Trust Document

The most important rule relating to the duties of a trustee is that requiring them to obey the directions in the trust deed both with regard to the interests of the beneficiaries (i.e. who is entitled to what) and with regard to the administration of the trust (managing the trust property). Trustees are also subject to very strict standards as to the way in which their powers and discretion may be exercised.

5.6. Fiduciary Relationship of Trustee

The courts regard a trust as creating a special relationship, which places serious and onerous obligations on the trustees. Thus the law regards the special "Fiduciary" relationship of a trust as imposing stringent duties and liabilities on the person in whom confidence is placed - the trustees - in order to prevent possible abuse of that confidence. A trustee is therefore subject to the following rules:

(a) **No private advantage**

A trustee is not permitted to use or deal with trust property for private direct or indirect advantage. If necessary the court will hold him personally liable to account for any profits made in breach of this obligation.

(b) **Best interests of beneficiaries**

Trustees must exercise all their powers in the best interests of the beneficiaries of the trust.

(c) **Act prudently**

Whether or not a trustee is remunerated he must act prudently in the management of trust property and will be liable for breach of trust if, by failing to exercise proper care, the trust fund suffers loss. In the case of a professional the standard of care which the law imposes is higher. Such trustees hold themselves out as having special expertise in trust work and therefore the courts will expect them not simply to act prudently but to exercise skill of a very high standard. Failure to exercise the requisite level of care will constitute a breach of trust for which the trustee will be liable to compensate the beneficiaries. This duty can extend to supervising the activities of a company in which the trustees hold a controlling shareholding.

5.7. Advantages of a Trust

Trusts are a powerful tax-planning tool but they also have many other uses, which are of equal if not greater importance. It may be particularly important for those who have set up confidential offshore accounts or companies to consider using a trust to transfer those assets after death. A fact, which is not well publicized, is that Swiss banks hold vast assets in suspense accounts because those assets cannot be claimed by their legal heirs. Accounts were set up and maintained in strict confidence in order to avoid taxation. On death it can be highly inconvenient, if not impossible, to claim those assets under the probate procedure of a will because to do so would reveal the existence of the assets and may trigger a charge to inheritance tax, many years of avoided income tax interest and other penalties. These amounts due to the taxman may come to more than the value held within the account! The same considerations can apply to the shares of an offshore company. A trust can be used to hold a bank account or the shares of an offshore company and these problems can then be avoided. A properly drafted and managed trust can confer advantages under any or all of the following heads:

(a) **Asset protection**

Trusts can be used very effectively to protect assets. In simple terms, assets transferred to a trust no longer form part of the property owned by the settlor and therefore if the settlor experiences financial problems the trust assets cannot be grabbed by the creditors of the settlor. Those assets would therefore be protected if the settlor experienced financial difficulties due to bankruptcy, dissolution of marriage or a court award made as a result of, for example, a professional negligence claim. Thus, although the settlor may be declared insolvent a portion of his assets might be safeguarded by the trust structure and could therefore be used to maintain the family of the settlor otherwise. This premise is legally correct but is an over-simplification of the law. Under certain circumstances it is possible for an aggrieved creditor to have the transfer of the assets into trust set aside by showing that the settlor set up the trust with the intention of avoiding a current or future liability or because the relevant debt arose within a specified time after the transfer into trust. In effect, it has hitherto been difficult to know that the assets transferred into trust are completely safe from creditor attack. It was for this reason that many of the more astute offshore jurisdictions created what is generally referred to as the concept of the "asset protection trust" by initiating legislation which provides that as long as the transfer into trust is made at a time when the settlor does not have notice of any impending claim against those assets then as soon as the assets are correctly placed into trust they are absolutely safe from future attack. By choosing an offshore jurisdiction, which has initiated "asset protection legislation", it is possible to gain a degree of additional protection over and above the already considerable asset protection inherent in a normal trust structure. It is therefore important to set up the trust in an offshore jurisdiction, which has initiated such legislation in order to guarantee the maximum security for the trust assets.

(b) Tax planning

Assets transferred into a suitably drafted offshore trust structure are, in simple terms, no longer considered as belonging to the settlor and therefore the income and capital gains generated by those assets are taxed according to the rules in the country of residence of the legal owners - the trustees. Inheritance tax would normally be eliminated because the trustees would not die upon the death of the settlor. Anti-avoidance legislation in the home country of the settlor may operate to reduce the effectiveness of a trust for tax planning purposes but, generally speaking, trusts can be extremely effective for tax planning purposes and a correctly structured and administered trust will produce substantial savings in income tax, capital gains tax and inheritance tax/estate duty.

(c) Avoiding the expense and delays of probate

The death of the head of the family wills usually result in major disruption of the family estate whether or not there is a will. In most common law jurisdictions the estate must go through the probate procedure with much consequential delay, expense, publicity and upheaval. By establishing a trust probate can be avoided because the fact of death will have no effect on the trust property which will continue to be held and managed in confidence by the trustees in accordance with the terms of the trust.

(d) Confidentiality

The probate procedure mentioned above is, essentially, a public procedure. The relevant home country tax authorities will need to receive a complete list of all the property owned by the deceased in order that that property can be assessed for estate duty and in order that the property can be legally transferred to the executors who may then distribute to the legal heirs of the deceased according to the will. This procedure is therefore entirely unsuitable for those who wish to keep details of their assets confidential. If a confidential offshore structure has been set up during lifetime then revealing the existence of that offshore structure during the probate procedure may have considerable negative tax consequences. It may therefore be wholly inappropriate to include those offshore assets within the will. If a will is not to be used to transfer assets then the only other legal form of transfer is via a trust which would generally serve to save estate duty and to keep the trust assets confidential.

(e) **Avoiding forced heirship**

In non-common law jurisdictions there will often be questions of forced heirship to consider i.e. the deceased will not be permitted to leave his property to anyone he wishes on his death. This is a particular problem in continental European countries and other civil law jurisdictions as well as in countries of Islamic tradition. A trust can be used to overcome the problem of forced heirship but care is needed in selecting a jurisdiction for the trust, which has an appropriate trust law.

(f) **Estate planning**

Many people do not want their assets to pass outright to their heirs, whether chosen by them or as prescribed by law, and prefer to make more complicated arrangements. These might involve providing a source of income for a widow for life, making provision for the education of children or providing a fund to protect members of the family in the event of sudden illness or other disasters. A trust is probably the most satisfactory and flexible way of making arrangements of this kind.

(g) **Protecting the weak**

A trust provides a vehicle by which a person can provide for those who may be unable to manage their own affairs such as infant children, the aged, the disabled and persons suffering from certain illnesses.

(h) **Preserving family assets**

Preserving the family assets or increasing them is often a motive for setting up a trust. Thus, an individual may wish to ensure that wealth accumulated over a lifetime is not divided up amongst the heirs but retained as one fund to accumulate further, with provision for payments to members of the family as the need arises while preserving some assets for later generations.

(i) **Continuing a family business**

A person who has built up a business during a lifetime will often be concerned to ensure that it continues after death. If the shares in the company are transferred to trustees prior to death a trust can be used to prevent the unnecessary liquidation of a family company. The terms of the trust will ensure that the individual's wishes are observed. These might include provision for payments to be made to members of the family from dividend income received by the trustees but that the trustees retain the shares and keep the company running save in special circumstances justifying sale of control or liquidation. This may be particularly advantageous where the family members have little business experience of their own or where they are unlikely to agree on the correct way to manage the business.

(j) **Gaining flexibility**

The best-laid plans can, in a changing world, rapidly become obsolete. A discretionary trust can, however, be structured to provide for a system of management of property that is capable of rapid change as circumstances demand.

5.8. Selection of the Jurisdiction

There are many jurisdictions, both onshore and offshore, in which it is possible to set up a trust. When choosing the correct jurisdiction it is important to select one which has a strong tradition of enforcing trusts, has an English Common Law system, has an established reputation for trust business, has enacted modern legislation which embraces the newer concepts of trusts - particularly asset protection - and imposes low or no tax on the trust. In the light of these requirements, the onshore jurisdictions such as the UK, USA and Australia are unsuitable because of the high tax that they would visit upon the trust structure.

Other jurisdictions are not recommended because of political uncertainties e.g. Hong Kong. Others because they have only recently started to attract trust business and therefore their courts and professionals have only limited trust experience e.g. Mauritius, Cyprus, Nevis etc. Other jurisdictions, whilst being noted for their trust expertise, have not kept pace with the modern trends in legislation which give additional benefits and additional protection to trust assets - surprisingly many of the more traditional trust jurisdictions fall into this category such as Jersey and Guernsey.

There is a very wide choice of jurisdiction and only a small number of those jurisdictions are able to offer all the important elements and can therefore be said to be the best available. Although there are other jurisdictions which offer similar advantages like Gibraltar, the Turks & Caicos Islands or Isle of Man.

Gibraltar and the Turks & Caicos Islands, in particular, have initiated strong asset protection legislation and have a requirement that a professional trustee is licensed. Trust companies must therefore prove to the relevant licensing authority that they have the necessary probity, experience, financial resources, management methods and professional indemnity insurance to ensure that they can set up and administer trusts in a totally proper and professional manner.

5.9. Offshore Trusts - Alleged Disadvantages

(1) Irrevocability

It is not correct that trusts once set up cannot be revoked. Trusts can be made revocable but this usually has tax, estate duty, asset protection and stamp duty disadvantages. Revocability is a matter to be discussed when the terms of the trust are considered.

(2) Loss of control of property

Many potential settlors are reluctant to transfer property to trustees because they fear loss of control over that property. In other words there are many who like the idea of a trust but wish to continue to exercise effective control over the trust assets despite the transfer to the trustees. However, careful planning together with an understanding of the fundamental legal requirements of a trust is required if the trust is to remain valid. If too much control is retained over the assets there is a risk that the trust will not be effective and the person who set up the trust will continue to be regarded by the law as the owner and all the advantages of having the assets held in trust may be lost. In particular, a court may force a settlor to exercise any control he retains in a particular manner thereby negating any asset protection advantage, which would otherwise have existed. Despite this there are devices which may be used to give comfort to a settlor:

(a) **Letter of Wishes**

When setting up a discretionary trust it is common for the settlor to indicate to the trustees by letter or otherwise how the settlor would have dealt with those assets if he had retained the necessary control. Such a letter will not be binding on the trustees, and therefore has no adverse consequences, but in practice most reputable trustees would be reluctant to deal with the trust property in any way other than that suggested by the settlor except, for example, where a change in circumstance or other matters suggests it is clearly disadvantageous to the beneficiaries to act in that manner.

(b) **Protector**

It is possible for a protector to be appointed who exercises some degree of control over the trust property. In our opinion, it is unwise for the protector to be given anything other than negative powers as this may mean that the protector is considered to be a quasi-trustee and negative consequences may result especially when the protector is resident in a high tax country. Thus, for example, the protector's powers should be limited to vetoing the decisions or actions of the trustees rather than having power to force the trustees to act in any particular way. For example, the trust deed may stipulate that no distribution from the trust can be made by the trustees without the consent of the protector but the trust deed should not give the protector power to instruct or force the trustees to make a distribution. The needs for the protector to be consulted are structured without a protector being appointed. It is usual for a trusted friend, family relative or professional adviser of the settlor to be appointed as the protector but it is becoming increasingly common to use the services of a professional trust company to act as protector.

(c) **Two Tier Company and Trust Structure**

Greater flexibility can sometimes be achieved by having the underlying assets owned by a company whose shares are owned by a suitable trust -rather than having the underlying assets owned directly by the trust. The settlor, or an appointee of the settlor, may act as the director of the company and may therefore exercise day to day control over the underlying assets with minimal interference or need to refer to the trustees. This two tier structure may have tax and other disadvantages where the director of the company is resident in a high tax country but can be used to good effect in certain circumstances.

(d) **Joint Trustees**

There is no reason why a trust could not be structured so that there are joint trustees with the agreement of both trustees being required in order to take any action. The second trustee may be the settlor himself, or a corporation controlled by the settlor. Again, there may be negative tax or other consequences resulting from such a structure or if the settlor is resident in other than a low tax jurisdiction but this is a solution worth considering. Alternatively, a check and balance may be obtained by having two different professional trust corporations acting as joint trustees. This can be cumbersome and expensive but may be suitable for certain trusts.

(e) Self Administered Trust Companies

It may be possible for a settlor to establish his own trust company, which acts as trustee of his trust. If tax savings are a primary motive for establishing the trust this will rarely be a suitable solution except in cases where the settlor and his family are resident in an offshore or low tax jurisdiction but may be a possibility where the tax considerations are irrelevant. Correctly structuring the ownership of the trust company can often be problematical so this structure has yet to gain widespread popularity but may be worthy of consideration.

(f) Hybrid Companies

A hybrid company is a company, which is limited by shares and guarantee and therefore has both shareholders and members. The directors and shareholders control the company but have no rights to receive benefits. The members have no control but hold the rights to benefit from the company assets. Thus the shareholders are analogous to the trustees and the members are analogous to the beneficiaries. The "Settlor" transfers assets to the company but retains the shares and makes his family the members. In this way he can pass on benefits without losing control. With this solution problems can arise upon the death of the shareholders as, unless great care is taken, there ceases to be an effective way of administering the company. The ideal solution is to place the shares under the control of a suitable trust company but, of course, this will result in no more controls for the "Settlor" than he would have using a traditional trust structure.

(3) Costs

Many believe that the costs of running a trust are prohibitive. Whilst it is true that many of the major banks and other financial institutions will make hefty charges for setting up a trust and will then expect to receive a percentage of the trust assets in annual administration fees, the level of fees charged by the smaller independent trust companies are generally much more reasonable and make the advantages of setting up a trust available to those with even relatively modest estates. Independent trust companies are also able to offer a more personalized service and also benefit from the fact that they are truly independent and can therefore select the best investments for the trust without being under pressure to place trust money with their own in-house investment advisers - see the section entitled "Accountability of trustee" for further explanation on this important point.

VI
Typical
Jurisdictions

6.1. Andorra

Nestling high in the Pyrenees, between France and Spain, measuring no more than 465 km 2, Andorra has preserved its neutrality and its identity through more than 700 years with a unique record of diplomatic non-involvement in European affairs. The elected local government consisting of Cap de Govern (President) and his ministers (28) directs government from la Casa de la Vall (the Houses of Parliament). In 1993, Andorra created its own constitution and is now a member of the United Nations. The French and Spanish governments, the two Co-Principe's retain responsibility over military defense and extreme foreign affairs. The Principality is a no tax jurisdiction with any direct taxation being levied on income, capital or corporations. Wealth and inheritance taxes do not exist. The population of Andorra is 60,000 from which 20,000 are native Andorran. The official language is Catalan, but Spanish and French are widely spoken and accepted. The economy of Andorra is split between farming, banking, financial services and tourism, with over 12 million tourists visiting the country every year. The Principality is an ideal location in which to site management and control of offshore companies. Banks offer a wide range of professional, discreet and confidential services with banking secrecy being upheld by law. Andorran companies can be established for local trade, asset and investment holding and cross-border commerce. There

are two types of Andorran companies, both of which enjoy limited liability. The Societat Limitadad (S.L.) is a company often used for local
trading and must have a paid up share capital of at least ESP 1,000,000
(Spanish Pesetas). The Societat Anonima (S.A.) is usually established
for businesses, which enjoy a much higher turnover and must have a
minimum paid up share capital of ESP 5, 000, 000.

**The Andorran Societat Limitadad (S.L.) has the following
characteristics:**

- There are no corporate taxes whatsoever.
- A minimum of two shareholders is required and at least one shareholder must be of Andorran nationality owning a minimum of
67% of the companies share capital. Non-Andorrans and non-residents can only own 33% of the share capital. Details of shareholders are kept at the local registry. An offshore company can be used
to own 33% of the share capital. It is possible to arrange for an
Andorran citizen to act in a nominee capacity for the ultimate
owner of the company.
- The share capital must be fully paid up in advance of incorporation. This amount must be deposited with an Andorran bank in a
designated company incorporation type account. The bank must
then release a special certificate, addressed to the designated notary,
responsible for concluding incorporation formalities.
- Annual accounting information and books must be maintained at
the companies registered office, but these need not be audited or
filed with local authorities.
- Names must end with S. L. It is advisable that the chosen name be
at least Catalan sounding.

6.2. Anguilla

Anguilla is the most northerly of the Leeward Islands and is located approximately 950 miles south east of Miami, Florida. There is an estimated population of 9,000 and a land area of 36 square miles. The Island is a British Dependent Territory with a legal system based upon English Common Law with local modifications. The Island is governed by an Executive Counsel of ministers appointed from the Legislative Council of locally elected members presided over by a British appointed Governor. Britain maintains responsibility for defense and foreign affairs. Communications are excellent. Currency is the EC Dollar but the US Dollar circulates freely and there are no foreign exchange controls.

The Anguillan International Business Company (IBC):

- Anguillan IBC's are formed pursuant to the International Business Companies Ordinance of 1984 which includes all the most desirable aspects and features of this modern type of legislation. The Anguillan IBC is an extremely flexible product which provides for minimal reporting, no requirement to file financial statements, no requirements to disclose beneficial ownership, no requirement to hold meeting on the islands and provides that meetings may be held in person, by telephone or by other electronic means.
- Anguilla is a major no tax haven. There are no direct taxes such as income tax, corporation tax, capital gains tax, profit tax, gift tax or death duties.
- An exempted company need only have one shareholder and shares can be issued in bearer or registered form. There is no requirement to file the details of shareholders on any public record.
- A minimum of one director is required and corporate directors are permitted. There is no requirement to file the details of directors on any public record.
- There is no requirement to file accounts or an annual return. The only annual requirement is that the company must pay the relevant

fee to the local government on the anniversary date of incorporation.

- The following words cannot be used either in English or any other language: Assurance, Bank, Building Society, Commonwealth, Co-operative Society, Fidelity, Friendly Society, Guarantee, Indemnity, Insurance, Re-insurance, Trust, Trustee, Underwriter, Royal, Imperial, Empire, Municipal and Chartered or any derivatives of any of those words without the written consent of the relevant department of the local government department. The name of an IBC must indicate that the company is limited.

- As a matter of local company law the company MUST maintain a registered office address within Anguilla and MUST also appoint an Anguillan resident as registered agent. The Confidential Relationships Ordinance of 1981 makes it an offense punishable by a maximum fine of US$ 10,000 for anybody to reveal confidential information, including details of the owners and directors, about an Anguillan IBC company.

6.3. Bahamas

The Bahamas are a group of around 700 islands located off the southeast coast of the state of Florida, USA and have been an independent member of the British Commonwealth since 1973. The Bahamas have one of the oldest parliamentary democracies in the Western Hemisphere and the islands have a political and legal system, which closely follows the UK system, and British common law applies. The population is approximately 255,000 centered principally on the capital city of Nassau on the island of New Providence. The Islands boast excellent communications with a state of the art telephone system and convenient flight links to most major international air routes. The Bahamas have an excellent range of international banks based in the islands with currently 396 banks holdings licenses under the Banks and Trust Companies Regulations Act 1965. Confidentiality is excellent with the

English common law duty of confidentiality being preserved and expanded upon by statute imposing penalties upon banks, attorneys, auditors and government officials who are privy to private information. Additionally, the Bahamas have no tax treaties or agreements for the exchange of information with any other state except agreements covering mutual assistance in cases of drug trafficking.

The International Business Company (IBC):
In January 1990 the Bahamas introduced the International Business Companies Act, which allows for companies to be quickly and easily incorporated for the purpose of transacting offshore business. Such companies have the following characteristics:

• IBC's pay no taxes in Bahamas.
• A minimum of one shareholder is required and either registered or bearer shares may be issued. No details of the shareholders appear on the public file but a register of shareholders must be kept at the registered office address of the company in Bahamas.
• A minimum of one director is required and corporate directors are permitted. Details of the directors do not appear on the public file.
• No annual return or accounts need be filed. It should be noted that penalty fees of up to 50% of the annual license fee would be incurred if the license fee is not paid when due.
• Names must end with one of the following words, or abbreviations thereof - Limited, Corporation, Incorporated, Societe Anonyme or Sociedad Anonima. The following words, and their associated activities, cannot be used: Assurance, Bank, Building Society, Chamber of Commerce, Chartered, Cooperative, Imperial, Insurance, Municipal and Royal.
• As a matter of local company law the company MUST maintain a registered office address with the Bahamas and must also appoint a Bahamas resident as registered agent.

• There are no specific statutory provisions governing secrecy in relation to companies but English Law, which applies within the jurisdiction, does impose a common law duty on professionals to keep the affairs of their clients confidential.

6.4. Belize

Belize (formerly British Honduras) is an independent democratic Commonwealth country located on the Caribbean seaboard of Central America. Since independence from Britain in 1981, it has enjoyed a stable and democratic Government. The cabinet, under the leadership of the Prime Minister directs the policy of the Government, which consists of the Prime Minister and ministers chosen by him from an elected House of Representatives and an appointed Senate. Although there are fairly high rates of tax for resident persons and companies in Belize, it now offers tax-free IBC's by virtue of the IBC Act 1990. This legislation is modeled on the earlier British Virgin Islands legislation and as the annual Government fees are only $100, whereas the equivalent fee payable in BVI is US$ 300. Belize is likely to become an important offshore corporate domicile.

The Belize IBC:
• IBC pay no taxes in Belize.
• A minimum of one shareholder is required and either registered or bearer shares may be issued. No details of the shareholders appear on the public file but a register of shareholders must be kept at the registered office address of the company in Belize.
• A minimum of one director is required and corporate directors are permitted. Details of the directors do not appear on the public file.
• No annual return or accounts need be filed. It should be noted that penalty fees of up to 50% of the annual Government fee will be incurred if the license fee is not paid when due

- Names must end with one of the following words, or abbreviations thereof - Limited, Corporation, Incorporated, Societe Anonyme or Sociedad Anonima The following words, and their associated activities, cannot be used: Assurance, Bank, Building Society, Chamber of Commerce, Chartered, Cooperative, Imperial, Insurance, Municipal and Royal.
- As a matter of local company law the company must maintain a registered office address within Belize and must also appoint a Belize resident as registered agent.
- There are no specific statutory provisions governing secrecy in relation to companies but English Law, which applies within the jurisdiction, does impose a common law duty on professionals to keep the affairs of their clients confidential.

6.5. Bermuda

Bermuda remains today the oldest colony of the United Kingdom yet it has been self-governing with respect to its own affairs, aside from defense and external affairs, for over 300 years. At the same time because of its strategic location in the North Atlantic (being much further north than is commonly believed and considerably closer to New York and Boston than the Caribbean) Bermuda benefits from being effectively under the US defense umbrella. The legal system is based on English common law, modified and supplemented by Acts passed under the Bermuda Constitution Order, 1968. Bermuda is governed by the locally elected House of Assembly but ultimate authority lies with the Queen who is represented by the Governor. With a population of close to 60,000 and a thriving tourist industry, Bermuda enjoys communications and travel connections of a high standard. Bermuda has attracted substantial insurance business and, after London and New York, Bermuda enjoys the third largest premium flow of any insurance center. Bermuda is of interest to Hong Kong people looking for an area to establish an offshore company because the Hong Kong Stock Exchange has approved the Bermuda Exempted Company for listing purposes.

The Bermuda Exempted Company:

- The Exempted Company will receive an undertaking from the Minister of Finance that the company will not be subject to any tax or duty on profits or income capital, gain or appreciation and that no inheritance tax or estate duty will be payable on shares debentures or other obligations of the company. Currently the exemption extends until 2016 but it may be further extended at a later stage.
- A minimum of one shareholder is required and bearer shares are not permitted. The beneficial ownership of the company must be revealed to the Government at the time of incorporation but such details are given in confidence. The share register of the Company is open to inspection by the general public but anonymity can be retained through the use of nominees. NB - bank references must be provided on the proposed beneficial owners of all Bermuda companies. These references must be provided by Banks where the individual has had a personal banking relationship for a minimum of three years.
- A minimum of 3 directors is required and there must be sufficient directors ordinarily resident in Bermuda to allow for a quorum to be present. Meetings of directors and of shareholders may be held outside of the island. A register of Directors and Officers must be maintained and this register is open to inspection by the general public.
- No annual return of shareholders is made although underlying beneficial interests are disclosed to the Government at time of incorporation. The requirement to have annual audited accounts may be dispensed with by unanimous decision of the directors and shareholders.

- A minimum issued - as distinct from paid-up - capital of US$ 12,000 is required in the case of exempted companies. If the company is not conducting insurance business there is no minimum amount for paid-up capital.
- As a matter of local company law the company must maintain a registered office address within Bermuda, must appoint a Bermuda resident company secretary and must also appoint a quorum of Bermuda resident directors (i.e. a minimum of 2 directors must be resident in Bermuda).

6.6. British Virgin Islands

The British Virgin Islands are a British dependency located in the Eastern Caribbean, about 80 kilometers East of Puerto Rico. English is the official language and the official currency is the United States Dollar. The Government is stable and promises to remain that way. There is good commercial and professional infrastructure and the Government is actively encouraging the development of the offshore finance business and has now upgraded the Companies Registry by installing state of the art technology. The International Business Companies Act was passed in 1984 and created the International Business Company (IBC) which is the preferred offshore company vehicle. In recent years the BVI has become extremely popular, particularly in the Far East region, due to the extensive marketing of the jurisdiction particularly by lawyers who moved from Panama during the Noriega regime and set up offices in the BVI.

The BVI IBC:
- IBC's pay no taxes in BVI.
- A minimum of one shareholder is required and either registered or bearer shares may be issued. No details of the shareholders appear on the public file but a register of shareholders must be kept at the registered office address of the company in.

- A minimum of one director is required and corporate directors are permitted. Details of the directors do not appear on the public file.
- No annual return or accounts need be filed. It should be noted that penalty fees of up to 50% of the annual Government fee would be incurred if the license fee is not paid when due.
- Names must end with one of the following words, or abbreviations thereof - Limited, Corporation, Incorporated, Societe Anonyme or Sociedad Anonima. The following words, and their associated activities, cannot be used: Assurance, Bank, Building Society, Chamber of Commerce, Chartered, Cooperative, Imperial, Insurance, Municipal, Royal and Trust.
- As a matter of local company law the company must maintain a registered office address within BVI and must also appoint a BVI resident as registered agent.
- There are no specific statutory provisions governing secrecy in relation to companies but English Law, which applies within the jurisdiction, does impose a common law duty on professionals to keep the affairs of their clients confidential.

6.7. Canada

Canada is an English speaking commonwealth country in which an English legal system applies. Canada is not generally perceived as a place in which it is possible to establish a non-resident, non-tax paying type of company and therefore the Canadian non-resident company provides a very low profile and extremely useful tax planning vehicle. Canadian law treats all companies incorporated in Canada as resident for tax purposes and taxable on worldwide income. In addition any company, wheresoever incorporated, which is controlled and managed from Canada is also treated as Canadian tax resident and taxable on worldwide income. These facts would seem to preclude the possibility of establishing a non-taxable company in Canada but certain Canadian provinces have corporate statutes which provide for the continuation of existing foreign corporations in Canada and a Canadian non-resident company can thereby be established by taking a foreign company, registering that company in Canada and ensuring that the central management and control of that company takes place outside Canada. Under these circumstances the company would be deemed by the Canadian tax authorities to be neither incorporated nor managed and controlled from Canada and not therefore subject to Canadian taxation on non-Canadian source income. One of the provinces within Canada, which allows for such entities to be established, is Alberta where extra-provincial registrations may be achieved under the Business Corporations Act.

Canadian Non-Resident Company Structure:

- Provided that the continued Canadian corporation is managed and controlled from outside Canada then only Canadian source income would be taxable in Canada i.e. as long as the activities of the company took place outside of Canada and no Canadian source income was thereby generated then such a corporation would not be subject to Canadian tax.
- The corporate structure would follow that of the place of incorporation of the original company and therefore if a TCI company was used only one shareholder would be required. Details of the shareholders would not appear on public file in TCI but would appear on the public file in Canada. However, confidentiality can be retained by issuing shares to bearer or by using nominee shareholders.
- Again the structure of the company follows the original incorporation and with a TCI company only one director is required. Details of the directors do not appear on the public file in TCI but do appear on the public file in Canada. Therefore, confidentiality can only be retained by appointing third party directors.

- Tax returns in Canada would have to be filed even if they showed that no Canadian source income had been generated and therefore no tax was payable. Accounts need to be prepared and accounting records maintained at the Canadian office of the company although companies with assets of less than 5 Million Canadian Dollars do not need to have their accounts audited.
- Names must not be misleading or denote any connection with the Canadian authorities or British Crown. Names containing words such as "Insurance" or "Bank" would require prior authorization and proper licenses to be obtained before they could be used.

6.8. Cayman Islands

The Cayman Islands are a British colony situated in the Caribbean Sea approximately 500 miles South of Miami, Florida. The Islands enjoy sophisticated legal, accounting and banking services and derive political stability by virtue of their connection with Britain. The legal system is British and the government is headed by a Governor appointed by the Crown who presides over a Government made up of twelve locally elected members and three senior civil servants who hold ex-officio office. There is no exchange control and no restrictions on the movement of funds to or from the Islands. The Confidential Relationships (Preservations) Law makes it a criminal offence for any person to divulge confidential information to a third party and the Cayman Islands have no double taxation treaties with any other part of the world but have undertaken to assist foreign governments by giving them information where a Cayman Island Company has been used or involved in activities which are mutually considered as criminal. Tax offences would not be covered by this treaty so no information would be revealed where allegations of tax offences are made.

There are two types of Cayman Islands company:
1. Cayman Exempt Companies

2. Cayman Ordinary Non-resident Companies

1. The Cayman Islands Exempt Company:

- There are no taxes in the Cayman Islands on income, capital gains, profits, dividends, investments or capital transfers. The company receives a twenty-year guarantee against taxation from the Cayman Islands Government, which may be extended, to thirty years on application.
- Bearer or registered shares are permitted. Details of the shareholders are not maintained on public record.
- Details of the directors must be advised to the company registrar but this information is not available for public inspection. Directors do not have to be resident in the Cayman Islands but one statutory meeting of the directors must be held within the islands every year. This may be done more conveniently by the appointment of proxies. A minimum of one director is required. Corporate directors are permitted.
- There is no requirement to file accounts with the registrar. However, an annual return must be filed. The return takes the form of a simple declaration.
- Names must end with one of the following words, or abbreviations thereof - Limited, Corporation, Incorporated, Societé Anonyme or Sociedad Anonima. The following words, and their associated activities, cannot be used: Assurance, Bank, Building Society, Chamber of Commerce, Chartered, Cooperative, Imperial, Insurance, Municipal and Royal.
- As a matter of local company law the company must maintain a registered office address within the Cayman and must also appoint a Cayman resident as registered agent.
- The Confidential Relationship (Preservation) Law makes it a criminal offence to divulge confidential information or to willfully obtain or attempt to obtain confidential information relating to a

Cayman Island company. The Law imposes a maximum penalty of a fine of CI\$ 5,000 and/or a term of imprisonment of up to 2 years.

2. The Cayman Ordinary Non-Resident Company:

Generally, the alternative to an Exempt Company is an Ordinary Non-Resident Company. Whether or not the company is resident or non-resident is a matter of status and is not determined by the residency or otherwise of the directors and shareholders. For a company to be resident (or "local") it must fulfil various immigration criteria and therefore such companies are not suitable for international operations but the ordinary non-resident company provides a useful and cheaper alternative to the exempt Cayman company. An Ordinary Non-Resident Company has the following characteristics:

- A non-resident company is not subject to taxation within the Cayman Islands.
- Bearer shares are not permitted. Corporate shareholders are permitted. Shareholders may be resident or non-resident in the Islands. Unlike the exempt company, however, the Companies Law does provide that any member of the public may inspect the register of an ordinary company at the registered office. Thus confidentiality can only be guaranteed through the use of the nominee shareholders.
- Details of the directors must be advised to the company registrar but this information is not available for public inspection. Directors do not have to be resident in the Cayman Islands but one statutory meeting of the directors must be held within the islands every year. This may be done more conveniently by the appointment of proxies. A minimum of one director is required. Corporate directors are permitted.
- An Annual Return must be made setting out details of any change in the ownership of the shares in the company's capital. Additionally it should be noted that the Register of Members is

available for public inspection at the company's Registered Office. The Register of Directors is not so available.

- There are no restrictions on the use of words in the name of an exempt company as long as it does not give the impression that the company is undertaking banking, trust, insurance or company management business. The words "Building Society", "Chamber of Commerce" and any words suggesting, in the opinion of the Registrar, Royal patronage, or connection with any society or body incorporated under the Royal Charter may not be used. An ordinary non-resident company must include the word "Limited or "Ltd." after its name.

6.9. Cook Islands

The Cooks Islands are a group of 15 islands situated in the South Pacific Ocean, approximately due West of Tahiti and due South of Hawaii. The largest island and administrative center is Rarotonga. The Islands became self-governing in 1965 but New Zealand retains responsibility for external affairs and defense. The Government of the islands is carried out by a locally elected parliament consisting of 24 members but executive authority still remains with Her Majesty, The Queen of England in her capacity as head of the Commonwealth. The legal system is common law and is closely based on applicable statutes of England. English is widely spoken within the islands. Communications are excellent and both New Zealand and local currency are legal tender.

The Cook Islands International Company:
- International Companies are not subject to any form of Cook Islands taxation.
- A minimum of one shareholder is required and bearer shares are permitted. No details of shareholders appear on the public file.
- A minimum of one director is required and corporate directors are permitted. Details do not appear on public file.

- A brief annual return must be filed but no accounts have to be lodged.
- There are a few restrictions on the names which can be used for incorporation in the Cook Islands but the following words and their associated activities cannot be used without prior authorization and/or licensing: Assurance, Bank, Building Society, Chamber of Commerce, Chartered, Cooperative, Imperial, Insurance, Municipal and Royal.
- As a matter of local company law the company must maintain a registered office address within the Cook Islands and must also appoint a Cook Islands resident as registered agent.

6.10. Cyprus

Cyprus is an island situated in the northeastern Mediterranean Sea at the crossroads of Europe, Asia and Africa. The capital city is Nicosia, which has a population of about 200,000 people. Cyprus gained independence from Britain in 1960 and adopted a presidential system of Government with elections for the President taking place every 5 years. In 1974 Turkey invaded Cyprus and has since occupied the northern 40% of the island although discussions are currently taking place with a view to reunification of the island. The official languages are Greek and Turkish but English is widely spoken and is the language mostly used in business, government and the courts. Laws are based on the English legal system and company law is modeled on the UK Companies Act 1948. In addition, Cyprus has signed an associate agreement with the European Union. Communications are excellent.

A Cyprus Offshore Company:

A Cyprus "offshore" company is defined as an otherwise normal Cyprus company which is owned by non-residents of Cyprus and does business mainly outside the islands. Such a company has the following characteristics:

- Tax is levied on worldwide income at a rate of 4.25% on profit. As such, Cyprus is a low tax country rather than a no tax country. However, one of the great benefits of Cyprus companies is that Cyprus has signed a good range of tax treaties which provide for reduced or zero withholding taxes on dividends, interest and royalties paid to a Cyprus company. Treaties have currently been concluded with Austria, Bulgaria, Canada, China, Czechoslovakia, Denmark, France, Germany, Greece, Hungary, India, Ireland, Italy, Kuwait, Norway, Poland, Romania, Russia, Sweden, United Kingdom, United States, and Yugoslavia. Further treaties are currently being discussed with Belgium and Finland.
- A minimum of two shareholders is required and details appear on the public file but anonymity can be retained by the use of nominee shareholders. Bank references on the beneficial owners must be submitted to the Central Bank of Cyprus but these details are protected by secrecy laws. Bearer shares are not permitted.
- A minimum of one director is required and details appear on the public file but anonymity can be retained by the use of third party directors. There is no legal requirement that the directors be Cyprus resident but in order to obtain relief under the taxation treaties signed by Cyprus it is likely that the company would need to be seen to be Cyprus resident and therefore have a majority of the directors based in Cyprus.
- An annual return which gives details of all those who have held shares throughout the year and the current directors must be filed. In addition, every Cyprus company must prepare audited accounts and submits these to the Central Bank and the income tax office.
- Names must end with the word "Limited". The following words and their associated activities can not be used: Assurance, Bank, Building Society or any other words deem sensitive or offensive. As a matter of local company law the company must maintain a registered office address within Cyprus and must also appoint a

company secretary who, for practical reasons, must be resident in Cyprus.
- Although details of the shareholders and directors appear on the public file, details of the beneficial owners supplied to the Central Bank are protected by statutory secrecy provisions.

6.11. Delaware

Delaware is a small state situates on the East Coast of the United States of America, often referred to as the "Gateway to the United States". Marked by few regulations and a lack of bureaucracy in arranging its affairs and with the Delaware Corporation Law being considered throughout the US among the most attractive for organization purposes, it is a valuable jurisdiction in which to organize new companies. The policy of Delaware courts has always been to construe the Corporation Law liberally, to interpret any ambiguities or uncertainties in the working of the Statutes so as to reach a reasonable and fair construction. This causes the careful investor to have confidence in the security of the investment. Corporations not having any business in Delaware pay no Delaware corporate income tax. Franchise tax compares favorably with other states and is payable on the authorized share capital of a company at a rate of 1%. It should be noted however that Delaware corporations do fall within the Federal Tax System.

A Delaware corporation has the following characteristics:
- This is covered above, but it should also be noted that shares owned by non-residents are free from all taxes, including State Inheritance Taxes.
- A minimum of one shareholder is required and bearer shares are not permitted. A minimum of one director is required and there is no restriction on his nationality. The offices of President, Vice-President and Treasurer may be vested in the sole director.

- A franchise tax report must be completed each year showing details of the officers of the corporation. However accounts need not be filed.
- Corporation names must end with one of the following words, or abbreviations thereof - Association, Company, Corporation, Club, Foundation, Fund, Incorporated, Institute, Society, Union, Syndicate or Limited. The following words, and associated activities, cannot be used bank, trust, university, college or school.

6.12. Gibraltar

Gibraltar is a peninsula with an area of 2.75 square miles situated at the Southern most tip of Spain. Gibraltar has been a Crown Colony of the United Kingdom since 1713 when the Territory was ceded to Britain under the terms of the treaty of Utrecht. Gibraltar is politically and economically stable and although Spain still maintains a territorial claim over Gibraltar the British Government has undertaken not to place the people of Gibraltar under the sovereignty of another state without their free and democratic consent. This consent is most unlikely to be forthcoming. Britain maintains responsibility for defense and international affairs but local matters, including company and taxation law, are the preserve of a locally elected House of Assembly. Gibraltar is a full member of the European community having been included as a member when Britain joined in 1973 but Gibraltar is specifically excluded from the European Common Agricultural Policy, the VAT system and the Common Customs Union. Gibraltar enjoys a sophisticated range of banking, legal, accountancy and other professional services. Communications are excellent. The currency is, for all practical purposes, the British Pound Sterling (although local Gibraltar Pounds are also issued and trade on a par with Sterling) and the population is bilingual in English and Spanish which facilitates the translation of documents for the Spanish speaking market.

The Gibraltar Tax Exempt Company:

A company incorporated in Gibraltar which is owned by non-residents of Gibraltar and does not transact business with other Gibraltar resident companies or individuals is eligible to apply for tax exempt status in Gibraltar. Upon successful application issued with a certificate, which guarantees exemption from Gibraltar taxation for a period of 25 years provided that the company complies with the conditions of tax exempt status and pays an annual duty to the Gibraltar Government of £225 p.a. At the end of every year the exempt company must file a statement attesting to the fact that the company has complied with the conditions applicable to its exempt certificate. An exempt company is convenient to administer due to the fact that it may have locally appointed directors and may maintain Bank accounts within Gibraltar. Thus the whole of the administration may be located within Gibraltar which helps to prevent the assumption that the company may be tax resident anywhere else.

A company, which is incorporated in Gibraltar, owned by non-residents of Gibraltar and managed and controlled by directors who reside and hold their board meetings outside of Gibraltar will be considered as non-resident. A non-resident company is not subject to Gibraltar corporation tax except on that part of the profit, which is remitted to Gibraltar. In practice this means that a non-resident company may be totally exempt from Gibraltar corporate taxation provided that it does not maintain Bank accounts within Gibraltar.

The Non-Resident-Company is cheaper as it is not subject to the fixed rate annual duty and other fees which are payable by the exempt company (see fee comparison below) but it is generally less convenient to manage due to the requirement to appoint non-resident directors and maintain Bank accounts outside of Gibraltar only. This may have tax implications in the home country of the directors. The shares of a non-resident company would be subject to Gibraltar estate duty whereas the shares of an exempt company would not. In a world of ever changing fiscal legislation the 25-year guarantee enjoyed by the exempt company may prove particularly useful in the future. In addition to the above types of non tax-paying companies Gibraltar offers two further types of company structure which may be extremely useful in a tax planning exercise:

The Gibraltar-Qualifying-Company is similar to the exempt company but, instead of being non-tax paying, the company elects its own rate of tax as long as that rate is 2% or above. This type of company can be useful where it is necessary to show that a certain minimum level of taxation has been paid in order to gain relief from taxation in another country. For example, the taxation systems of certain countries provide that if taxation above a certain minimum level has already been paid on income remitted to the home country then no further taxation will be charged on those profits by the home country. The qualifying company can therefore elect to pay the required minimum level, which would allow that income to be remitted to the home country without further taxation being suffered on arrival. A Qualifying Company must lodge an amount of £1,000 with the Gibraltar Government as a guarantee against payment of future taxation.

The Gibraltar-1992-Holding-Company was specifically created to take advantage of European Union Directive 90/435. In simple terms, this Directive states that dividends may be paid by a subsidiary company located in one EU state to a parent company located in another EU state without the imposition of withholding tax as long as the recipient parent company is not capable of being exempt from tax. The prohibition against tax exemption would mean that the exempt and non-resident Gibraltar companies are not suitable to receive dividends from a subsidiary in another EU State so the 1992 Holding Company was created. The 1992 Holding Company pays 35% tax on all profits except on dividend income received. Dividends paid out of the 1992 Holding Company are subject to a 1% withholding tax. This type of company can be particularly advantageous for non-EU countries who are investing within the EU and are expecting to receive dividend income. As can be seen the effective rate of tax on that dividend income will be 1% when remitted out of Gibraltar or zero tax when held within Gibraltar.

Gibraltar companies have the following characteristics:

- Gibraltar companies must have a minimum of one shareholder who may be corporate or individual. Details of shareholders appear on the public file but anonymity can be preserved by the use of nominee shareholders. Bearer shares cannot be issued.
- Gibraltar companies must have a minimum of 1 director who may be corporate or individual. Details of the directors appear on the public file but anonymity can be preserved by the use of third party directors.

An annual return must be filed each year showing details of shareholders and directors. Exempt and non-resident companies do not have to file accounts on the public file but the Qualifying 1992 Holding company would need to prepare audited account to the Gibraltar tax authorities.

- The following words and their associated activities are restricted: association, royal, imperial, trust, trustee, bank, assurance, group, Europe and international.
- As a matter of local company law the company MUST maintain a registered office address within Gibraltar. Additionally, it is a requirement, practical in the case of a non-resident company and legal in the case of the other types of Gibraltar Company.

6.13. Guernsey

Guernsey is the second largest of the Channel Islands with Jersey being the largest. Guernsey lies in the English Channel off the north West Coast of France. It covers 24 square miles and has a population of approximately 58,000 with the principal center of business activity being St. Peters Port. The Channel Islands have a unique constitutional arrangement with the UK. The Islands are possessions of the English Crown as distinct from colonial and overseas dependencies of the United Kingdom and accordingly the locally elected legislative assemblies have the exclusive right to legislate on matters of domestic concern to the Islands (including taxation) whilst the United Kingdom Home Office is responsible for the external affairs of the Islands. The Islands are associated members of the European Community and as such are only subject to European law in so far as they specifically contract in to the European Community. Thus they have elected to become part of the common tariff and agricultural levy system but are not subject to European law in most other areas. The official language is English although French is still spoken and the legal system is based upon a mixture of English and French law. Guernsey has signed double taxation agreements, which provide for the exchange of information with the United Kingdom so UK residents should carefully consider whether Guernsey is the correct place in which to set up an offshore structure.

Companies which are incorporated in Guernsey but which are owned by non-residents of Guernsey and do no business with Guernsey resident individuals or corporations can be granted exempt status in Guernsey.

Such companies have the following characteristics:
- Guernsey exempt companies pay no taxes in Guernsey but are subject to a flat rate corporate duty of £500 per annum irrespective of profit.
- A minimum of two shareholders is required and corporate shareholders are permitted. Please note that details of the beneficial owner of the company must be communicated to the Guernsey authorities but that information is protected by secrecy provisions. Bearer shares are not permitted. A share register must be maintained at the registered office address of the company and must be available for inspection by any member of the public. Details of shareholders are also maintained on the public file at the

Companies Registry but anonymity can be preserved by the use of nominee shareholders.

- A minimum of one director is required and corporate directors are permitted. Details of directors must be kept at the registered office and appear on the public file kept at the Companies Registry but anonymity can be preserved by the use of third party directors. There is no requirement to have resident directors.

- An annual return which gives details of the current directors and shareholders and any change in the shareholders since the last return or, in the case of a company filing its first annual return since the date of incorporation, must be filed at the public registry in January of each year and a filing fee of £100 is payable. It should be noted that fines are payable if a company fails to file its annual return on the due date.

- Names must end with the word "Limited". The following words and their associated activities can not be used: Assurance, Bank, Building Society or any other words deemed sensitive or offensive.

- There are no specific statutory provisions governing secrecy in relation to companies but English Law.

6.14. Hong Kong

Hong Kong is located in the South China Sea 100 miles south east of Guanzhou (formerly known as Canton). There is an excellent range of professional services available as Hong Kong serves as the major business center for the whole of the Far East. The local currency is the Hong Kong Dollar which is freely interchangeable but has a pegged exchange rate against the US Dollar. There are no exchange controls. One of the major advantages of utilizing a Hong Kong company is that there is no immediate suggestion that the company is a tax avoidance vehicle as Hong Kong is major trading entity in its own right and the vast majority of the 50,000 Hong Kong companies incorporated annually are local trading companies doing real business in the region. It is possible to create a Hong Kong registered corporate entity in two different ways: (1) By incorporating a new Hong Kong company. (2) By registering an existing foreign company in Hong Kong under Part XI of the Hong Kong Companies Ordinance.

The Hong Kong Incorporated Company:
- The rate of taxation is 16.5% on Hong Kong source income only. In practice this means that, with careful structuring, as long as a Hong Kong company is not actually doing business in Hong Kong it would normally be possible to arrange the affairs of the company so that no tax would be payable.
- A minimum of two shareholders is required whose details are filed on the public register. Corporate shareholders are permitted and anonymity can be achieved by the use of nominee shareholders.
- A minimum of two directors is required and full details of these must be filed with the Public Registry. There is no requirement for board meetings to be held within Hong Kong and directors may be resident anywhere in the world.
- Hong Kong companies are required to file full audited accounts and must also prepare and file an annual return which gives details of the current directors and of the shareholders who have held shares in the company at any time during the year.
- Names, which suggest any connection to the UK head of state, are generally prohibited and certain words, which suggest specialist activity, can only be used when the appropriate licenses have been obtained e.g. bank, insurance company and other specialist financial enterprises.
- As a matter of local company law the company must maintain a registered office address within the jurisdiction of incorporation and must also appoint a local resident company secretary.

6.15. Isle Of Man

The Isle of Man is an English speaking country, which lies in the Irish Sea between Britain and Ireland. It occupies an area of 588 sq. km (277 sq. miles). Constitutionally it has never been part of the United Kingdom, but is rather a self-governing territory within the Commonwealth with a population of about 70,000 persons. Tynwald, the Isle of Man parliament, is responsible for the Island's domestic affairs including taxation. Britain is responsible for the Island's defense and foreign affairs. The Island has a special relationship with the European Community: whilst it is associated with the EC the Island is excluded from the Community's fiscal harmonization policy. The Isle of Man is a part of the UK V.A.T. area and does impose V.A.T. on goods and services. As such, an Isle of Man company may be registered for V.A.T. and may therefore prove a suitable vehicle for international trade with other member states of the European Union. The Isle of Man law is closely based on English common law and the decisions of the courts in England are regarded as being persuasive in the Manx courts.

The Isle of Man offers 2 distinct types of non-tax paying company:

1) A Non-Resident-Company is a company incorporated in the Isle of Man, which is owned, managed and controlled by persons who reside outside of the Isle of Man. Upon the filing of a non-resident declaration, the company will not be subject to Isle of Man taxation. Instead will pay a fixed rate non-resident company duty of £600 per annum irrespective of magnitude of profits. The duty is payable in the first year upon the filing of the declaration and annually thereafter on the filing of the annual return on the anniversary of the company's incorporation.

2) An Exempt-Company must be owned by non-residents and must have at least one Manx resident director and a professionally qualified company secretary. Exempt status can be obtained provided that the company's business and trading is carried on out-

side of the Isle of Man. Banking activities may be controlled from within the Island and any income and profit derived from the account will not be subject to Isle of Man taxation. The exempt fee payable to the Isle of Man Government is £300 per annum, payable in the first year upon application and annually thereafter before 30th June.

An Isle of Man company has the following characteristics:

- Isle of Man exempt and non resident companies are not subject to any form of tax on profit in the Isle of Man but do pay a flat rate annual fee to the Isle of Man Government which is £600 for the non resident company or £300 for the exempt company.
- A minimum of 1 shareholder is required which may be an individual or a corporate body. Details of the shareholders must be filed on the public file but anonymity can be preserved by the use of nominee shareholders.
- Each Isle of Man company requires a minimum of two directors and corporate directors are not permitted. Details of the directors must be filed on the public file but anonymity can be preserved through the use of third party professional directors. It is important to note that an exempt company must have at least one Isle of Man resident director and would usually have all its directors resident to clearly demonstrate that the control and management of the company takes place on the Isle of Man. This is not a requirement for a non-resident company, which may have non-resident directors.
- An annual return must be filed each year showing details of shareholders and directors. There is no requirement to file accounts with the registrar, but please note that resident companies do need to produce accounts for the tax authorities.
- The following words cannot be used without further approval; bank, assurance, casualty, guarantee, indemnity, insurance, re-insurance,

surety, underwriting, bank, trust, trustee, holdings, international, group.

- As a matter of local company law the company must maintain a registered office address within the jurisdiction of incorporation. Exempt Isle of Man companies must, as a matter of law, appoint an Isle of Man resident professionally qualified company secretary as well as a local director. For resident and non-resident Isle of Man companies it is a practical but not legal requirement to appoint an Isle of Man company secretary.

6.16. Jersey

Jersey is the largest of the Channel Islands and lies in the English Channel off the north West Coast of France. The population is approximately 75,000 with the principal center of business activity being St. Helier. The Channel Islands have a unique constitutional arrangement with the UK. The Islands are possessions of the English Crown as distinct from colonial and overseas dependencies of the United Kingdom and accordingly the locally elected legislative assemblies have the exclusive right to legislate on matters of domestic concern to the Islands (including taxation) whilst the United Kingdom Home Office is responsible for the external affairs of the Islands. The Islands are associated members of the European Community and as such are only subject to European law in so far as they specifically contract in to the European Community. Thus they have elected to become part of the common tariff and agricultural levy system but are not subject to European law in most other areas. The official language is English although French is still widely spoken and the legal system is based upon a mixture of English and French law. Jersey has signed double taxation agreements, which provide for the exchange of information with the United Kingdom and with Guernsey so UK residents should carefully consider whether Jersey is the correct place in which to set up an offshore structure.

A Jersey Exempt Company:

Companies which are incorporated in Jersey but which are owned by non-residents of Jersey and do no business with Jersey resident individuals or corporations can be granted exempt status in Jersey.

Such companies have the following characteristics:

- Jersey exempt companies pay no taxes in Jersey but are subject to a flat rate corporate duty of £500 per annum irrespective of profit.
- A minimum of two shareholders is required and details appear on the public file but anonymity can be retained by the use of nominee shareholders. Please note that details of the beneficial owner of the company must be communicated to the Jersey authorities but that information is protected by secrecy provisions. Bearer shares are not permitted.
- A minimum of one director is required. Corporate directors are not permitted. Details of directors must be kept at the registered office and are disclosed to the Registrar, but do not appear on public file. Further anonymity can be preserved by the use of third party directors.
- An annual return, which gives details of all current shareholders, must be filed at the public registry in January of each year. It should be noted that fines are payable if a company fails to file its annual return on the due date.
- Names must end with the word "Limited". The following words and their associated activities can not be used: Assurance, Bank, Building Society or any other words deemed sensitive or offensive.
- As a matter of local company law the company must maintain a registered office address within Jersey and it is normal practice and a practical but not legal requirement for a Jersey resident company secretary to be appointed.

6.17. Labuan

The Federal Territory of Labuan comprises seven small Islands of which Pulau Labuan is the largest. Labuan lies off the North West Coast of Borneo and not far from Brunei. At its nearest point, Labuan is only some 10 kilometers from the Coast of the East Malaysian State of Sabah. The official language is Bahasa, Malaysia, however, English is widely spoken and many documents and publications are available in English. The official currency is the Malaysian Ringgit although the majority of offshore companies in Labuan are required to carry on business in a foreign currency. Labuan is part of Malaysia and responsibility for its administration falls directly under the Prime Ministers Department. On the 6th November 1989, the Government of Malaysia declared Labuan an International Offshore Financial Center and the Offshore Companies Act was enacted on 1st October 1990. Malaysia has signed 32 double taxation treaties with various countries. It is conceivable under tax rules that a Labuan offshore company may be Malaysian resident and therefore benefit from the provisions of a particular tax treaty. Whilst professional advice should be sort at the time of incorporation it is assumed that an offshore company electing to pay 3% tax on audited net profits would be considered tax resident in Malaysia.

The Labuan Offshore Company:

A Labuan offshore company shall only carry on business in, from or through Labuan. An offshore company may not carry on business with a resident of Malaysia except as permitted by the Offshore Banking Act 1990 and may not carry on the business of banking or insurance.

A Labuan offshore company has the following characteristics:

- An offshore company may elect to pay either 3% tax on audited net profits or pay a flat rate of RM 20,000 per annum which would negate the requirement to appoint an auditor and file audited financial statements.

- The minimum number of shareholders required is one. Details of shareholders are not available for inspection by the public. No resident of Malaysia, other than a trust company or a domestic or foreign company granted a license might hold shares in an offshore company.
- A minimum of one director, either corporate or individual is required. Directors do not have to reside in Labuan. Details do not appear on the public file.
- An offshore company must have at least one resident secretary who must be an officer of a licensed Labuan trust company. Additional secretaries who are not resident in Labuan may be appointed.
- An annual return must be lodged annually, not later than 30 days before the anniversary of the date of the companies incorporation. As dealt with above a Labuan offshore company can dispense with the requirement to file annual audited accounts so long as the members of the company resolve at a general meeting not to appoint an auditor. In this case an offshore company can elect to pay a flat rate of tax of RM 20,000 per annum or the same amount as an annual registration fee. If, however, the offshore company intends to take advantage of the 3% tax on audited net profits then accounts must be audited by an approved auditor and filed.
- Offshore companies are allowed to have names in a foreign language, provided they use Roman characters and the letter L as part of its name.
- An offshore company must maintain a registered office, resident secretary and where applicable must maintain accounting records in Labuan.

6.18. Liberia

Liberia is situated on the West Coast of Africa and covers a land area of over 43,000 square miles. It has a population of approximately 2,000,000. Its capital, Monrovia, is the center of the country's

Government and commercial activities. The Liberian dollar has the same value as the US dollar, which freely circulates there, and there are no currency regulations or exchange controls. The Republic of Liberia was founded in 1845 and has, since its establishment, enjoyed independence and a stable free enterprise economy. The legislature consists of a Senate and a House of Representatives. The country adopted a new constitution in 1985, following a military coup d'etat in April 1980 and elections for a President and both Houses were held in November 1985. The official language of commerce and government is English. The country enjoys reasonable economic stability. It has long term investments in the rubber, iron ore and timber industries by both foreign and domestic interests.

A Liberian company has the following characteristics:
- Provided that no more than 25% of the voting powers of the company is resident in Liberia, and all income derives from outside Liberia, the company will not be subjected to any income tax. There is, however, an annual fee of US $150 payable to the Liberian authorities.
- Only one shareholder is required. Bearer shares are permitted. Details of shareholders do not appear on public file.
- A Liberian company requires three directors, who will be named in the Articles. However, there is no need to register changes in directors. There is no residential qualification imposed in respect of directors.
- There is no requirement to file accounts, or a requirement for the company to appoint Auditors. No returns are required to be filed.
- Any name is acceptable for a Liberian company, provided it is not identical to an existing company. The name must include the words "Limited" or "Corporation", but their equivalent in certain languages is permissible.

- As a matter of local company law the company must maintain a registered office address and a registered agent in Liberia.

6.19. Liechtenstein

Liechtenstein lies in the region of the upper Rhine between Switzerland and Austria, about 75 miles (a 90 minute drive) each of Zurich, Switzerland which as the nearest International airport. It is Europe's fourth smallest state with an area of approximately 100 square miles. Vaduz is the capital and the seat of Government. Liechtenstein, like its neighbors, is politically neutral. It is a constitutional hereditary monarchy with a Prince as head of State and a democratically elected parliament. The legal system is based on civil law. The total population is 28,000 of which 18,000 are citizens of the Principality. The official language of Liechtenstein is German, although English is widely spoken amongst the business community. The Swiss Franc is the official currency and there are no exchange controls. Banking and financial services are one of Liechtenstein's main industries and within this industry there are high levels of secrecy with heavy sanctions imposed for any breaches of confidentiality. On an international comparison Liechtenstein has very well protected bank confidentiality

The Liechtenstein Family Foundation:
The foundation is typically formed purely for family reasons, non profit and non-commercial reasons since a foundation is not suitable for the pursuit of commercial business. A foundation is commonly used to hold assets, fixed property and shares in other companies.

A Liechtenstein family foundation has the following characteristics:
- A Liechtenstein Foundation is not subject to any form of income tax, capital tax, transfer taxes or inheritance taxes in Liechtenstein.
- The Liechtenstein nominated settlor is required to appoint a Board of Directors and these details appear on the public file at the Liechtenstein Registry. It is a legal requirement that there is at least

one Liechtenstein individual board member however, additional directors are permitted and these may be of any nationality or residence and can either be individuals or corporate entities.

- The by-laws, better known as the wishes of the beneficiaries are normally drawn up with assistance by the Settlor. These details are not available on public record and details of this document need only be held at the premises of the Registered Agent located in Liechtenstein. It is important that the by-laws clearly state what the wishes of the beneficiaries are and what should happen in the event of demise. The by-laws are perhaps the most important instrument and form an integral part of the Foundation. It is important that people seek legal advice before the by-laws are finalized.
- The registered agent is required to file the Capital tax to the Liechtenstein Registry every year, but a family foundation that does not actively trade is not required to file audited accounts.
- The minimum nominal capital (Foundation Fund) is SF 30,000 or the equivalent value in any desired legal currency. Before the Foundation is established it is a legal requirement to pay up the nominal capital in advance and the nominal capital amount must be paid into a Liechtenstein Bank. The Liechtenstein bank must give a certificate to the Liechtenstein Registry to verify that the required capital has been paid up for the purpose of creating a foundation.
- The name of the Foundation must be registered with the Liechtenstein Registry. It is not permissible in Liechtenstein to use place names, state name, country names or well-known international names.

6.20. Luxembourg

The Grand Duchy of Luxembourg is situated in Western Europe between Belgium, France and Germany and was created within the German Bund by the treaty of Vienna of 1815. In 1867 Luxembourg gained independence from Germany and organized itself as a constitutional monarchy with the legislative power vested in a democratically elected parliament. Luxembourg is a member of OECD, the European Union, the Benelux Union and the Belgium/Luxembourg Economic Union. The capital city is also called Luxembourg and is the center of government, business and finance. The legal system is based on napoleonic code and is therefore similar to the Belgium and French legal systems. Population is approximately 400,000, 20% of whom are foreign nationals. French, German and English are widely spoken and used in business circles with French being the administrative language. The currency is the Luxembourg Franc which is freely tradable but there are approximately FLUX 30 to US$ 1. The maximum rate of corporation tax applicable to Luxembourg companies is 33% but additional municipal taxes can bring the aggregate rate to as much as 39%. There are, however, two types of companies to which special tax regimes apply and which are therefore useful for tax planning purposes:

The Luxembourg Holding Company:
A Luxembourg holding company is exempt from all forms of Luxembourg taxation but its activities are restricted to the holding of shares and certain other investments. In particular the company may not advance funds to its shareholders, invest in commodities or futures or carry out any sort of commercial or industrial activity. The company may only hold property in so far as it is necessary for its own use but could, for example, own the shares of a property investment company. This type of company is specifically excluded from the tax treaties signed by Luxembourg except the treaty signed by China.

The Luxembourg Societe De Participation Financiere (SOPARFI):
Luxembourg has recently extended its participation exemption regime and SOPARFI' s are now subject to the normal rate of national and municipal Luxembourg tax except that, subject to the fulfillment of certain conditions, dividends and capital gains are not taxed. Such compa-

nies are therefore able to take advantage of the EU parent/subsidiary directive 90/435 A SOPARFI is not excluded from the scope of the tax treaties concluded by Luxembourg and this may make this type of company extremely attractive for certain tax planning exercises. Luxembourg has signed tax treaties with most EU countries, Canada, Czech Republic, Hungary, Japan, Korea, Morocco, Norway, Slovak Republic, Switzerland and the US.

Both of the above types of Luxembourg companies have similar corporate characteristics:

- Profits taxation is dealt with above but the Holding Company pays an annual subscription tax equal to 0.2% of share capital and both types of company pay duty of 1% on the issue of new share capital. The minimum share capital is FLUX 1.250.000 and at least 25% of the authorized capital must be paid up. The holding company must have a minimum paid up capital of FLUX 1 million.
- A minimum of two shareholders is required. Details of the shareholders appear on the public file but bearer shares are allowed. However, if bearer shares are to be issued then the full amount of the authorized capital must be paid up on incorporation so if anonymity is required it is often preferable to use nominee shareholders.
- A minimum of three directors is required who may be corporate or individual. Details of the directors appear on the public file so anonymity may only be retained by appointing third party professionals to the Board.
- As a matter of Luxembourg law the company must maintain a registered office address with in Luxembourg and must also appoint a Luxembourg based statutory auditor.
- All Luxembourg companies must file full audited accounts and books of accounts must be maintained at the registered office and updated on a regular basis.

- Names must end with the word "Limited". The following words and their associated activities can not be used: Assurance, Bank, Building Society or any other words deemed sensitive or offensive.

6.21. Madeira

The Island of Madeira is situated in the north Atlantic Ocean about 700 kilometers off the coast of north west Africa on the same latitude as Casablanca. The Madeira archipelago, made up of the Islands of Madeira, Porto Santo and several small deserted islands, was discovered by the Portuguese navigators in the XV. Century and has been a Portuguese territory ever since. It is of interest to note that all the islands were completely uninhabited at the time of their discovery. Since 1976, due to political changes in Portugal, Madeira has been an autonomous region with its own Parliament and locally elected Government but Madeira is still legally and politically part of Portugal and is therefore a full member of the European Union. The local currency is the Escudo. Despite Madeira's autonomous status most of the Laws enacted by the Central Government and by the Portuguese Parliament are fully applicable in Madeira. Communications are good, the Island being served by an international airport with daily flights to mainland Portugal and frequent flights to other countries. Shipping is well served by deep-water ports at Funchal and Porto Santo, and the Islands telephone network is linked to mainland Portugal by cable and satellite giving easy, direct access to International networks. By legislation first put before the Portuguese Parliament as long ago as 1980 and enacted in 1986 the Madeira Free Trade Zone was established which gives substantial tax concessions to companies incorporated on the Island.

Madeira Companies:

Madeira companies, which are located within the Offshore Financial Center, can be structured so as to be completely exempt from all forms of Madeira taxation until 31st December 2011. Notwithstanding this attractive tax treatment, a Madeira company is considered to be the same as a normal Portuguese tax paying company and therefore falls within the terms of the taxation treaties signed by Portugal with Austria, Belgium, Brazil, Denmark, Finland, France, Germany, Italy, Japan, Mozambique, Norway, Spain, Switzerland and the United Kingdom. The terms of these treaties provide that payments from these countries can be made with a much lower rate of tax being withheld at source. For example, royalties being paid by an UK company to a non-resident corporation or individual would normally be subject to a with-holding tax of 25%. However, if those same royalties are paid to a Madeira company the rate of withholding tax may be reduced to 10% by virtue of the provisions of the UK/Portugal tax treaty. This is despite the fact that those same royalties would not be subject to tax on arrival within the accounts of the Madeira Company. In addition to the nor-mal offshore company, Madeira also allows for the incorporation of the SGPS. The SGPS has been specifically designed to take advantage of European Union Directive 90/435. The terms of that Directive require that dividends paid by a subsidiary located in one EU state to a parent located in another EU state must not be subject to any form of with-holding tax as long as certain conditions are met - the most important of which is that the parent company cannot be exempt from taxation in its country of incorporation. The SGPS is therefore subject to a rate of tax of 36% on dividends received from subsidiaries situated in other EU states but 95% of the dividend income is exempt from taxation. Thus, the effective rate of taxation on dividends is 1.8% only. The SGPS must not undertake activities other than holding shares in other companies. This type of company is therefore of considerable use to any company located outside the EU, which wishes to invest within the EU. Additionally, because the company is nominally subject to 36% tax, it would appear as though such a company would fall outside the provi-sions of the anti-tax haven legislation enacted by Japan. Under that leg-islation the profits of a foreign subsidiary of a Japanese company are taxed in the hands of the Japanese parent on a current year basis unless it can be demonstrated that the profits are subject to a rate of tax of at least 25% in the hands of the subsidiary. The Madeira SGPS would appear to fit this criteria and may therefore be extremely beneficial as an investment vehicle for a Japanese parent company.

The Madeira companies described above have the following characteristics:

- This is dealt with above but, by way of summary, a normal Madeira company is exempt from all forms of taxation until 31st December 2011. An SGPS pays tax at a rate of 36% on dividends received from EU subsidiaries but 95% of that income is exempt from tax making an effective rate of tax on those dividends of 1.8%. The SGPS is otherwise exempt from all tax.
- A minimum of one shareholder is required whose identity is a matter of public record. No share certificates are issued, the shareholding being described in the notarial deed when the company is set up or the structure altered.
- A minimum of one director is required who may or may not be a shareholder and, once again, whose details are on public record. Corporate directors are not permitted.
- As with all Portuguese companies, Madeira companies are obliged to file monthly or quarterly VAT returns and annual accounts in the Portuguese language and currency. An audit is only required for companies which have a substantial level of assets and turnover and/or large number of employees.
- Names end with the words "Limitada" or "Lda" and name clearance must be obtained through the Central Registry in Lisbon. Generally, names should be recognizable in the Portuguese language and restrictions would be imposed on names indicating involvement in banking, insurance and some financial services.

6.22. Malta

Malta is an independent republic, having gained independence from the United Kingdom in 1964, situated in the center of the Mediterranean Sea about 60 miles south of Italy and 180 miles north of North Africa. Government is exercised by a democratically elected parliament with elections being held every five years. Population is approximately 365,000. English and Maltese are the official languages but Italian is also widely spoken. English is the business language. Malta is a member of the Commonwealth of Nations and is an associate member of the European Union. Malta has also applied for full membership of the European Union and this application is currently under consideration. The legal system is based on the Napoleonic code but British Law has had a strong influence particularly in fiscal and commercial law. The official currency is the Maltese Lira (Lm). Malta has signed tax treaties with Australia, Austria, Belgium, Bulgaria, Canada, China, Cyprus, Finland, France, Germany, Hungary, India, Italy, Libya, The Netherlands, Norway, Pakistan, Poland, Sweden Switzerland, United Kingdom, and United States of America. At the beginning of 1996 Malta substantially revised its corporate law so as to remove the distinction between offshore and onshore companies and thereby hopes to guarantee that all Maltese companies will obtain favorable treatment under these tax treaties.

The Malta Company:

It was possible to register Maltese "offshore" companies up until the end of 31st December 1996 and such companies may continue to operate until 23rd September 2004 or ten years from the date of incorporation, whichever is the earlier. Offshore companies pay a fixed rate of tax of 5% on worldwide income. The new regime does away with the distinction between offshore and onshore companies and Malta now offers two types of company which will be of interest to the tax planner: The International Holding Company (I H C) and the International Trading Company

(ITC). These entities are taxed as described below and are designed to take advantage of the tax treaties signed by Malta. The ITC is statutorily defined as a company, which is engaged solely in carrying on trading activities from Malta with persons outside Malta and has objects expressly limited to such trading activities. The ITC may not hold foreign investments or equity. An I H C is a company whose activities are limited to foreign equity participation and other similar passive income generating activities. Such entities are taxed in a particularly advantageous manner where income is received from "participating holdings".

- I T C and I H Cs pay tax on their world wide income at a rate of 35% but there is a system of credit and refunds available to the shareholders which, in simple terms, reduces the net rate of tax to 4.2% in the case of I T C and between 0 and 6.5% in the case of I H C. This is an attractive system of taxation because the 35% rate is actually paid at the corporate level and it is thought that tax treaty benefits will thereby be assured.
- A minimum of two shareholders is required who may be corporate or individual. Details of the shareholders appear on public file but anonymity can be retained by the use of nominee shareholders.
- A minimum of one director is required, either corporate or individual, and details appear on the public file in Malta. In order to establish that the company is tax resident in Malta, and therefore to gain tax treaty benefits, it will be necessary to have the majority of the board of directors based in Malta.
- Companies must file an annual return and must also prepare audited accounts.
- As a matter of Maltese company law every Malta Company must maintain a registered office address in Malta and must also appoint a licensed Maltese "nominee company" as company secretary or sole director. The "nominee company" is legally liable for all actions of the Malta Company so will require to be involved fairly closely

in all business operations. Although there is no strict requirement that the director(s) be resident in Malta it is likely that tax treaty relief would not be afforded to any company which did not have a majority of directors resident in Malta. For most practical purposes it will therefore be necessary to appoint Malta resident directors.

- Confidentiality is governed by the Professional Secrecy Act, which has established a high common standard of confidentiality for all professional practitioners. Those who violate professional secrecy may be prosecuted under Section 27 of the Criminal Code and on conviction may be liable to a maximum fine of LM 20,000 and/or a 2-year prison sentence.
- Names must end with the word "limited". There are few restrictions on the words, which may be included within a company name but those indicating a connection with the banking or insurance industries can only be used when an appropriate license has been obtained.

6.23. Mauritius

Mauritius is a sub-tropical volcanic island situated in the Indian Ocean, approximately 2400 kilometers off the South East Coast of Africa and covers an area of 1,865 square kilometers. The population of the island is approximately 1.1 million comprising of people of Indian, African, Madagascan, European and Chinese origin. Due to its past history as a colony of both France and Britain, this population is largely bilingual in English and French. The official language is English while "Creole" is widely spoken in the island. The Republic of Mauritius is a Westminster style democracy headed by an appointed President. The President is the Head of State and Commander in Chief. The sixty members of Parliament are elected every five years by popular vote. Parliament is the legislative authority in Mauritius and is headed by the Prime Minister who is the Head of Government. Mauritius is one of the few countries with a hybrid legal system based on English and French law. The procedural law both in criminal and civil litigation is mainly English whilst the substantial law is mainly based on the French Napoleonic code. The Company Law is modeled on the English law. The highest court of appeal is the Privy Council in England.

There are two types of Mauritius company:
1. Mauritius International Company
2. Mauritius Offshore Company

1. International Companies

The International Companies Act 1994 was enacted to provide a comprehensive regime for the incorporation, regulation, operation and taxation of International Companies while maintaining the existing organization of the offshore business. This piece of legislation is extremely flexible and provides for a minimum of disclosure. Meetings need not take place in Mauritius, the objects may be unrestricted and there is no necessity to report changes in shareholders, directors and mortgages to the Registrar.

International Companies have the following characteristics:

- An International Company need only have one shareholder and shares can be issued in bearer or registered form. Details of the shareholders do not appear on the public file but there is provision for optional registration with the Registrar of International Companies.
- A minimum of one director is required and corporate directors are permitted. Details of the directors do not appear on the public file but there is provision for optional registration with the Registrar of International Companies.
- An International Company is not required to file either an annual return or accounts.
- The International Companies Act 1994 provides for the optional registration of the details of shareholders, directors and/or mortgages and charges. On incorporation an International Company

can elect whether to register any or all of these details or not. This election can be changed at a later date if desired. The registration details are not available for public inspection and are protected by the secrecy provisions referred to above but the Registrar of Companies may, on request from the registered agent, issue a certificate giving details of the registered particulars. The company is bound by the contents of that register but if desired the company could elect to cease registering such details by giving notice in writing to the Registrar.

- As a matter of local company law the company must maintain a registered office address within Mauritius and must also appoint a Mauritian resident as a registered agent.
- The Mauritius Offshore Business Activities Act 1992 requires that all information and documentation received be kept secret and confidential and imposes a penalty of a fine of up to 300,000 Rupees and imprisonment for a term not exceeding 8 years for failure to comply.
- The following words cannot be used in English or any other language: Assurance, Bank, Building Society, Chamber of Commerce, Chartered, Cooperative, Government, Imperial, Insurance, Municipal, Royal, State and Trust. International companies are prohibited from carrying on those activities engaged by offshore companies.

2. Offshore Companies

Offshore Companies, which were previously known as "Ordinary Status Companies", are formed under the Companies Act 1984 and regulated by the Mauritius Offshore Business Activities (M O B A) Act 1992. The substantial advantage offered by the Offshore Company is that it may be structured to be tax resident in Mauritius, even though it is not subject to Mauritius tax, and may thereby access the taxation treaties signed by Mauritius with the UK, France, Germany, Malaysia, Sweden,

India, Italy, China, Zimbabwe and South Africa. This makes it extremely attractive to invest in one of these countries through a Mauritius Offshore Company as taxation treaties provide that profits can then be withdrawn from that country either without the imposition of withholding tax or subject to a substantially reduced rate of withholding tax. The terms of the taxation treaty signed between Mauritius and India are particularly advantageous and the levels of taxation paid by a Mauritius Offshore Company making profits in India are considerably reduced from the normal levels of taxation which would be suffered by an individual or company investing directly in India. Additionally, after the profits have been removed from India then the Mauritius Offshore Company may hold those profits completely free of Mauritius taxation. India still imposes restrictions on investments in and out of the country and therefore requires that any investment into India by a foreign company or individual is approved by the Reserve Bank of India. Frequently the approval process takes a considerable length of time and results in onerous conditions being placed upon the investment. However, if a Mauritius auditor produces an Overseas Auditor's Certificate (O A C) stating that the investing company is an Overseas Corporate Body (O C B), which is defined as a company which is at least 60% owned by Non Resident Indians (N R I ' s), then the investment would normally be authorized speedily and without conditions. An N R I is defined as a citizen of India or a foreign citizen who has a parent or grandparent who was an Indian citizen and permanent resident of India at any time.

The benefits accruing to a Mauritius Offshore Company when used for investment in India may be summarized as follows:

Dividends paid by an Indian company to a non-resident would normally be subject to withholding tax at 25%. If those dividends are paid to a Mauritius Offshore Company then the rate of tax to be deducted is

5% if the Mauritius company owns more than 10% of the capital of the Indian company or 15% if less than 10% is owned.

Capital gains made from the sale of capital assets in India (e.g. shares, property etc) would normally be taxed at a rate of 55% for short term Capital Gains or 20% for long term Capital Gains but Capital Gains made by a Mauritius Offshore Company in India are completely exempt from tax. Capital Gains made on assets held for less then 12 months in the case of shares in a company or 36 months in the case of other assets are classified as short term otherwise all gains are classified as long term.

Royalty payments made out of India to a non-resident would normally be subject to a withholding tax of 30%. Royalty payments made by an Indian Company or individual to a Mauritian Offshore company would be taxed at the reduced rate of 15%.

Interest payments made by an Indian resident to a non-resident would be subject to withholding tax at a rate of 25%. If interest is paid to a Mauritius Offshore Company then, provided that the loan has been approved by the Indian Government, no tax need be withheld on those interest payments.

Offshore companies structured to take advantage of the taxation treaties signed by Mauritius must have the following characteristics:

- The normal rate of taxation for an Offshore company is 0% but the company may, if it desires, elect to pay a rate of tax of up to 35%. It may be desirable to elect to pay tax if, for example, the terms of a particular tax treaty require the Mauritius company to show that it is subject to a minimum rate of tax in order for the Mauritius company to obtain the relief provided for under that particular tax treaty. For most purposes this would not be required and the vast majority of offshore companies therefore elect to be exempt from all forms of taxation.
- The company must have at least 2 shareholders unless it is a wholly owned subsidiary. Bearer shares are not allowed. Details of the

shareholders must be reported to the Companies Registry and to the M O B A Authority but these details are not available for public inspection so confidentiality is assured. Please note that references and copy passports of the beneficial owners must be given to the M O B A Authority.

- A minimum of two directors is required and corporate directors are not permitted. A director is required to give his consent to act as director by filing form 4 with the Registrar of Companies but these details are not available for public inspection and are protected by the confidentiality laws. It is important to note that if the company wishes to access the taxation treaties then 2 Mauritius resident directors, who are approved by the M O B A Authority, must be appointed.

- Offshore Companies are exempted from filing an annual return with the Register of Companies but must file an audited profit and loss account and a balance sheet prepared in accordance with internationally accepted accounting standards but, again, the accounts are not available for public inspection and confidentiality is protected by the secrecy laws.

- The Mauritius Offshore Business Activities Act 1992 requires that all information and documentation received be kept secret and confidential and imposes a penalty of a fine of up to 300,000 Rupees and imprisonment for a term not exceeding 8 years for failure to comply.

- The following words cannot be used in English or any other language: National, Regional, State, Government, Authority, Corporation, Municipal, Chartered, Cooperative, Broadcast, Broadcasting, Diffusion, Rediffusion, Television and Chamber of Commerce. Banks and insurance companies must be licensed.

6.24. Netherlands

The Netherlands, more commonly known as Holland, is situated west of Germany and north of Belgium along the North Sea coast. It has an area of approximately 16,000 square miles and a population of approximately 15 million inhabitants making it the most densely populated country in Europe. The Netherlands is one of the most stable European countries and is a full member and one of the co-founders of the European Union. The official language is Dutch but English, German and French are widely spoken in the business community. The monetary unit is the Dutch Guilder (or Florin) which is divided into 100 cents, is freely convertible and is one of Europe's strongest and most stable currencies. The Netherlands is a constitutional and hereditary monarchy but executive power lies with the cabinet council presided over by the Prime Minister. Members of the cabinet council are formally appointed by the Queen and reflect the political majority of the second chamber of the Dutch Parliament which consists of 150 representatives directly elected for 4 year terms on the basis of proportional representation. The first chamber of the Dutch Parliament exists to review draft legislation, which has already been passed by the second chamber.

Tax Planning Through The Netherlands

The Netherlands can in no way be considered an offshore finance center. Corporate rates of tax are high: 37% on profits up to D F L 100,000 and 35% on the remainder and these rates apply to worldwide income. (In 1997 the top rate will be reduced to 36% and to 35% in 1998). However, concessionaire treatment of some forms of income coupled with the extremely wide network of double taxation treaties signed by The Netherlands (over 60 taxation treaties have currently been concluded including treaties with most of the major developed nations of the world) provide outstanding opportunities to use Netherlands corporations in structuring international financial transactions. Netherlands companies may be advantageously put to the following uses:

A. Holding Companies:

Subject to certain conditions a resident Dutch company may qualify for the "participation exemption" which exempts such companies from corporate tax on income and capital gains resulting from the holding or disposal of qualifying shareholdings.

B. Finance Companies:

The Netherlands imposes no withholding taxes on interest paid by a Netherlands company to a non-resident. Additionally, many of the Dutch tax treaties allow foreign companies to pay interest to a Netherlands company without a requirement to withhold tax or subject to a requirement to withhold tax at a reduced level. The Netherlands may therefore provide a suitable conduit through which inter-company loans may be made. The Netherlands require that the margin of profit on loans received and made must be (subject to a decreasing sliding scale) of between 1/6% and 1/8% for inter group loans and between 1/32% and ¼% on third party loans. The amount of this margin would be taxable at normal Dutch rates but the balance of the interest received will escape Dutch taxation.

C. Licensing Companies:

There is no withholding tax on royalty payments made by a Dutch company to a non resident and, as with interest payments, many of the tax treaties signed by The Netherlands allow foreign companies to make royalty payments to a Netherlands company without a requirement to withhold tax or subject to only a reduced rate of withholding tax. Where the Dutch company is related to the payee or payer then a margin on basis of a sliding scale ranging from 2%-7% (6% for lump sum payments and film royalties) must be maintained between the royalties received and the expenses paid out. The amount of this margin would be taxable at normal Dutch rates but the balance of the royalties received will escape Dutch taxation.

The Netherlands BV:

The Netherlands BV is the usual corporate vehicle to use for tax planning purposes. This type of corporate vehicle is similar in form to the UK limited liability company and therefore must impose restrictions on share transfers. Such a company has the following characteristics:

- As stated above, corporate tax is levied on worldwide income at a rate of up to 37% (36% in 1997 and 35% 1998) but exposure to corporate taxation may be kept to a minimum as described below. A particular attraction of using a Dutch company in an international tax planning exercise is that it is possible to obtain an advance ruling from the Dutch Revenue Authorities on the tax saving plan. Once granted, the ruling would generally be binding upon the Dutch Revenue for a period of four years with the possibility of further extensions for subsequent periods. This facility allows tax-planning exercises to be conducted with a degree of certainty, which is not generally available in other countries.

- A minimum of one shareholder is required and details appear on the public file but anonymity can be retained by the use of nominee shareholders. Bearer shares are not permitted. Share certificates are not issued but rather the shareholders details are entered into the corporate register. Shares can only be transferred by notarial deed.

- A minimum of one director is required and details appear on the public file but anonymity can be retained by the use of third party directors. There is no legal requirement that the directors be Dutch resident but in order to obtain relief under the taxation treaties signed by The Netherlands it is likely that the company would need to be seen to be Dutch resident and therefore have a majority of the directors based in The Netherlands.

- An annual return which gives details of all those who have held shares throughout the year and the current directors must be filed. In addition, every Netherlands Company must prepare audited accounts and submit these to the Central Bank and the income tax office.

- There are no secrecy laws in The Netherlands and, indeed, exchange of information may take place under the terms of the many tax treaties to which The Netherlands is a party.
- Names must end with the initials "BV". Names need not be in the Dutch language but must be in Roman script. Names should be sufficiently individual so as to prevent confusion with existing companies and names, which indicate an activity, are only acceptable if the implied activities are to be performed by the company.
- As a matter of local company law the company must maintain a registered office address within The Netherlands and must also register itself with a local Chamber of Commerce. For practical reasons a company must also appoint a local resident agent who will manage the affairs of the company in The Netherlands.

6.25. Nevis

The Island of Nevis in the Eastern Caribbean was a British Colony from 1628 until 1983 when it became independent and joined the Federation of St Kitts & Nevis and it is now a member of the British Commonwealth and the United Nations. Nevis has a democratic system of government based on the British parliamentary system with an elected local assembly. The legal system is based on British common law but the Nevis Business Corporation Ordinance, which was introduced in 1984, incorporates both British and US law with the Ordinance drawing heavily on the statute applicable in the US state of Delaware. The population of Nevis is approximately 9000. The local currency is the EC dollar which is worth approximately 2.7 US dollars. As with everywhere in the Caribbean, US dollars are widely accepted on the island. Nevis has an excellent telecommunications system, Cable & Wireless having installed a state of the art fiber optic digital system at the turn of the decade. There are no direct flights to or from Nevis to the US mainland or Europe but the island is easily accessible by utilizing connecting flights via Antigua. Nevis has a population of approximately 9,000. It has an excellent telecommunication system and although no direct flights are available to the Island from U.S.A. or Europe, can be reached by air using connecting flights via Antigua.

Nevis Corporation:
- A Nevis offshore corporation can operate completely fee of all forms of taxation.
- A minimum of one shareholder is required and shares may be issued in bearer form. Shares may have a value denominated in any currency or can be of no par value. There is no requirement for the details of shareholders to be registered on the public file.
- A minimum of one director is required and corporate directors are permitted. There is no requirement for the details of the directors of a Nevis Corporation to be registered on the public file.
- No annual return or accounts need be filed.
- Companies cannot undertake banking or insurance activities. However reinsurance activities are permitted and trust companies can be formed for private use.
- As a matter of local company law the company must maintain a registered office address within Nevis and must also appoint a Nevis resident as registered agent.
- The Confidential Relationship Act, 1985 operates to prevent the disclosure of confidential information and/or records and imposes maximum penalties of a fine of USD 50,000 and/or a twelve month prison sentence for the improper divulging or attempted or threatened divulgence of such information.

6.26. Niue

Niue is an independan, three hours flying time from New Zealand and 480 km from its nearest neighbor, Tonga. The Island is self-governed by a local assembly of 20 members, headed up by the Premier. New Zealand is responsible for defense and international affairs and Nuieans are New Zealand citizens. The official language is English. Offshore legislation was introduced in 1994 including an IBC Act, banking, insurance and trust legislation to enable the Island to offer a complete range of offshore products. The Island also has a planned tourism industry, which is developing steadily.

The Niue International Business Company (IBC):
Niue IBC's are formed pursuant to the International Business Companies Act of 1994 which allows for minimal reporting and maximum privacy. The Niue IBC can engage in any lawful business and can carry on transactions in whatever currency is preferred. There are no minimal or maximal capital requirements and mortgages and charges can optionally be registered if desired.

They have the following characteristics:
- IBC's are fully exempt from taxation on any activities carried on outside Niue and generally all transactions of an IBC are exempt from stamp duty.
- Shares may be issued in registered or bearer form and members can be natural persons or corporate bodies. Only one shareholder is required. No details appear on public record.
- A minimum of one director is required and corporate directors are permitted. There is no requirement to register the details of the first directors or any subsequent changes therein. Meetings can be held anywhere in the world.
- There is no requirement to file accounts or an annual return. Companies must though pay their annual license fee on time or penalties will be imposed.

- The name of the IBC must indicate that the company has limited liability by ending in Limited, Corporation, or any foreign equivalent approved by the Registry. The following words cannot be used: Assurance, Bank, Building Society, Chamber of Commerce, Chartered, Co-operative, Imperial, Insurance, Municipal, Royal or Trust Company, or any derivatives thereof, without prior approval.
- As a matter of local company law the company must maintain a registered office address within Niue and must also appoint a Nuiean resident as registered agent.
- There are no specific provisions governing secrecy but the common law duty of confidentiality owed by professionals to their clients applies.

6.27. Panama

The Republic of Panama occupies an area of 77,082 square kilometers and is situated between Costa Rica in Central America and Columbia in South America with coastlines on both the Pacific and Atlantic Oceans. Its capital, Panama City, is on the Pacific coast at the entrance of the Panama Canal. The country has a population of approximately 2 million of which 700,000 people live in Panama City. The Constitution of Panama provides for a Republican form of Government. Citizens over the age of 18 years have the right and obligation to vote directly for a President and two Vice Presidents, and to vote for appointment of Legislators to the Legislative Assembly. For the purpose of the election of Legislators, the country is divided into Electoral Circuits with an average of 30,000 voters in each. Panamanian law is based on the Spanish Civil Code, although the company law has been taken from the corporation law of Delaware in the USA. The official language is Spanish. Documents in a foreign language, which require to be filed at Companies Registry, must be accompanied by a Spanish translation. Equally company documents in Spanish are accompanied by an English translation. Spanish and English are used equally in business circles.

Panama City is linked by major scheduled airlines, through regular daily flights, with the principle cities of North, Central and South America, Europe and the Far East. It has excellent telecommunications and postal facilities, and courier services are well established in the country. The official currency is the Balboa, which, under a monetary agreement of 1904 with the United States, is at par with the United States dollar and is freely convertible. The US Dollar is also legal tender, and since there is no Panamanian paper currency it circulates freely. By use of nominee services, it is possible to protect the identity of the beneficial ownership of a company incorporated in Panama.

- Taxation in Panama is strictly territorial, and provided the company's activities are carried out outside of Panama no tax will be levied, other than a US $150 Annual Franchise Tax which is payable to maintain the good standing of the company.
- A company should have a minimum of two shareholders, and the names of the subscribing shareholders will appear on public record. These can, however, be nominees. Panamanian law does not require any details of any change in shareholders to be lodged after incorporation. Bearer shares are permitted.
- The directors of a Panamanian Company must appoint a President, Secretary and Treasurer. Whilst these offices may be held by one person, who is neither a director or a shareholder, the directors may equally appoint themselves. Details of the Directors must be registered on the public file.
- There is no requirement under Panamanian Law for a registered office to be maintained in Panama, but the company must maintain a Resident Agent who must be a Panamanian lawyer or a firm of Panamanian lawyers. The minute book of the company and stock register, which is required under Panamanian law, can be maintained in any part of the world. Provided no business is carried on within Panama there is no requirement to file returns with

the Panamanian authorities or to lodge any financial or other information unless the company is being wound up.

- Companies can be formed for all lawful objects and the name should terminate in the words Sociedad Anonima (or SA) or in a word in any other language which denotes that it is of limited liability ("Corporation", "Corp", "Incorporated", "Inc", "A.G." etc but not "Limited"). Words such as bank, insurance, re-insurance or trust cannot be used in any language.

6.28. Portugal

Portuguese legislation on foreign investment was significantly liberalized at the time of accession to the European Community and, apart from some sectors such as defense and public services, there are no restrictions on the percentage of foreign ownership allowed, it thus being possible to form a company which is totally owned by non-resident investors, whether corporate or individual.

There are various ways of establishing oneself in business in Portugal but in principle if one wishes to do business within Portugal then it is advisable to incorporate there. Indeed, resident entities normally receive more favorable treatment tax-wise than non-resident, especially with regard to withholding tax. Also, in practical terms and from a point of view of control it is advisable to have a permanent presence within the country. One further point is that if the commercial enterprise is part of an overall plan to establish residency, then such a residency request will only be considered if a permanent presence in Portugal is established.

Probably the best way of doing business in Portugal is through a Portuguese limited company. As opposed to operating in one's own name, a company has the advantage of limited liability, meaning that should the company incur debts only the share capital of the company is available to meet them. If one trades in one's own name then obviously all personal assets can be seized and used to meet debts.

The two principal forms of limited liability organization are the public company or corporation (Sociedade An—Nima - S.A.) and the quota company (Sociedade por Quotas - Lda.) and these are the most common corporate formations in Portugal for both foreign and national investors. However, other forms are possible and can be used, such as non-limited liability firms or mixed types of limited and non-limited liability companies or partnerships.

The Sociedade An—Nima is appropriate for larger and/or widely held enterprises and we concern ourselves here with the more common limited company suitable for small and medium sized enterprises.

The setting up of any corporate entity in Portugal depends upon two main steps: the signing of the articles of association at a notary and commercial registration of the same.

The minimum share capital prescribed by law is Escudos 400,000; the shares must have a minimum value of Escudos 20,000 and be divisible by Escudos 250. Since 31 December 1996, Single Shareholder Companies are permitted whilst until then a minimum of 2 shareholders were required. Share certificates are not physically issued, rather the shareholding is noted by way of a deed. Shareholders are jointly liable for all financing stipulated in the articles of association. Only the assets of the company itself are available to meet obligations to creditors.

There are no specific structures required for a quota company, which can have either one or more manager-directors appointed or a board of manager-directors. These managers may be chosen from non-members (i.e., non-shareholders) of the company.

A quota company may have an audit board or not. If there is no audit board, and if certain turnover, staff and total assets value limits specified by law are attained or exceeded during at least two years, then an auditor must be appointed.

After choice of the activity or objects to be pursued, definition of the future shareholders, and choice of the appropriate legal form of company, a number of procedures must be followed for the establishment of a business in Portugal, irrespective of the type of entity chosen. These are outlined as follow.

- Application requesting approval for the use of a company name and provisional tax card must be lodged with the Corporate Entities Registrar (Registo Nacional de Pessoas Colectivas). This requirement also applies to branches, which must use the same name as the parent company.
- The minimum share capital of the company to be set up (or a percentage of the same prescribed by law according to the form of the company, when the total capital exceeds the minimum capital required) must be deposited in a bank in an account opened in the name of the future company. This deposited share capital is retrievable once the company has been incorporated. The articles of association of the company previously drawn up must be signed by the shareholders in the presence of a Public Notary via a public deed.
- Registration with the tax authorities must be made by lodging a declaration of start of activity with the finance Department.
- Registration with the local Social Security office must be made within the period of one month after the start of activity.
- The company must be registered within the period of 90 days after the date of the deed with the Commercial Registry Office for the area in which the registered office of the company is situated. At the same time an application is forwarded by the local Registrar to the National Registry for the definitive tax contribution card to be issued.
- Publication of the articles of association in the official gazette and in a local newspaper. This will be handled by the Commercial Registry Office.

- The official books of the company, including the minute book, must be registered with the tax authorities and the Commercial Registry Office.
- When a company happens to have foreign employees it must apply to the Ministry of Employment for registration of their contracts of work.
- Special authorization concerning opening hours and extended or special periods of activity may be required for certain business activities.

Other Entities

Limited Liability Single Shareholder Company

(Estabelecimento Individual de Responsabilidade Limitada - EIRL)

A sole trader normally exposes himself to unlimited liability and thus is personally responsible for debt arising from his activities. By registering as a Sole Trader with Limited Liability (EIRL), only the assets of the establishment itself are available to meet any debts incurred in the course of business. In a bankruptcy, however, the assets of the single shareholder may also be called if it is proved that the basic principle of separation between the assets of the establishment and his own assets was not respected in running the business.

The registration process is the same as that for a quota company; the minimum capital prescribed by law is Escudos 400,000 and only one EIRL is permitted per person. It should be noted that since the Single Shareholder Company was introduced an EIRL could be changed into this type of company. This change must be made via a "Notarial Deed".

Branches And Representative Offices

It is possible to establish a branch in Portugal, whereby a foreign company is able to conduct normal business affairs. However, a branch does not constitute a separate legal entity and thus may not assume any legal responsibilities. Some of the advantages of a branch are:

- Exemption from with holding tax when profits are re-partied.
- **A simple form to operating than a subsidiary.**
- **Possibility of offsetting losses against domestic profits.**
- Free transmission of assets between home country office and branch, as there is no change in asset ownership.

The setting up of a branch does not require a notarial deed but registration is required with the Commercial Registrar of the area where the branch is to be situated for branches of foreign companies wishing to carry on business in Portugal for more than one year. Due to the fact that the Memorandum and Articles of Association (Incorporation Deed) of the foreign company have to be translated into the Portuguese language and subsequently published both in a local newspaper and the official Government Gazette, the establishment of a branch can be an expensive process.

In general there are no minimum or maximum limits on the amount of capital needed for setting up branches and the company is free to decide on what the capital needs of its branches are. However, the Commercial Registrar's office is unlikely to authorize the setting up of a branch with no capital assigned, and in practice a branch has to have as capital assigned at least the minimum of Escudos 400,000 required for the share capital of a quota company.

Apart from branches there are also other forms of representation that do not independently conduct business activities, acting instead as information channels for the head offices of the companies they represent, such as representative offices, agencies, etc.

6.29. Russia

- Incorporation Of A Company Of Limited Liability In Russia Wholly Owned By Foreign Physical Or Legal Entity
- The company name is acceptable in either Russian or English. If in Russian, the name will begin with the abbreviation A. O.

(Company Limited by Shares), and if in English, will be followed by the abbreviation J. S. C. (Joint Stock Company). The name cannot include the words "Insurance" or "Bank". A special license is required if the words "Moscow" or "Russia" are included in the name of the company.

- The minimum share capital of the company is 63,500,000 R.B.S, and there is no maximum capital. Fifty percent of the share capital should be paid up by or before the time of incorporation, with the remaining fifty percent payable within one year of the date of incorporation. Companies with high levels of capitalization require special permission from the Anti-Monopoly Committee of the Russian Federation.
- A company should have minimum of two shareholders, being either legal entities or persons. Their names appear on public records.
- There is a requirement for a registered office to be maintained in Russia.
- There is a minimum requirement of one Director. The Director or a Board of Directors (if more than one) must appoint a Chief Accountant. There is no maximum number of directors. The shareholders appoint a Company President, and the President is responsible for organization of Shareholders activity, holding meetings etc.
- A company must keep proper Books of Account in order to give a true and fair view of the state of the companies affairs and explain its transactions. Once a year a company must be audited. It will therefore be necessary to produce a full set of audited accounts to the Taxation Authority.
- The Russian Company may only have one current bank account, which must be held with a Russian bank. A minimum of two persons should be authorized to sign the account mandates/instruction (one of them being a Director and the other - Chief Accountant or his Deputy).

• The Russian Company will pay income tax at the rate of 32%. Federal and Municipal taxes, which vary according to the levels of capitalization are also levied. As the total taxation level is rather high, it is reasonable to use Russian companies as corporate representatives or agents, in order to reduce this fiscal burden

The following documents are required for the company incorporation:
(A) For legal entities:
1. Notarized copy of Memorandum and Articles of Association;
2. Notarized copy of a letter from the bank confirming that the legal entity has a bank account;
3. Notarized copy of Certificate of Incorporation;
4. Notarized copy of a Power of Attorney in favor of a certain person enabling him "to establish companies, sign documents and represent company interests on behalf of the Subscriber.

(B) For persons (acting as subscriber):
1. Notarized passport copy;
2. Notarized letter from his bank;
3. Notarized copy of Certificate of Registration as a businessman, or other reference showing business occupation, in the country of his residence. The above documents should be notarized and apostilled and produced in two copies or sets. One set will be translated into Russian and notarized.

6.30. Samoa

Samoa, which comprises of two large islands and several smaller isles, is situated in the center of the Southern Pacific Ocean, approximately equidistant between Honolulu and Sydney and immediately East of the International Date Line. Samoa has been a fully independent nation since 1962 and its constitution provides for a parliamentary Government, which combines the traditional Samoan social structure and a democratic voting system. The legal system of Samoa is based on English common law and incorporates a considerable body of New Zealand statute law due to the fact that prior to independence New Zealand was the administrating authority of Samoa. Population is approximately 162,000 of whom 90% are indigenous Polynesians. The balance of the population is of part Samoan and part Chinese or European extraction. Samoa has sophisticated international telecommunications system with telex, facsimile and international direct facilities via satellite. There are regular international flights to and from Australia, New Zealand and the surrounding Pacific Islands.

There are two types of Samoan Company:
1. Western Samoan International Company
2. Western Samoan Creditor Controlled International Company

1. Samoan International Company:
- ICs pay no taxes in Samoa.
- Normally a minimum of one shareholder is required and shares must be issued in registered form but details do not appear on the public register. Bearer shares are not permitted.
- A minimum of one director is required and corporate directors are permitted. Details do not appear on the public file.
- A brief annual return must be filed but no accounts need to be filed. It should be noted that penalty fees would be incurred if the license fee is not paid when due.
- Names must end with one of the following words, or abbreviations thereof - Limited, Corporation, Incorporated, Societé Anonyme or Sociedad Anonima. The following words, and their associated activities, cannot be used: Assurance, Bank, Building Society, Chamber of Commerce, Chartered, Cooperative, Imperial, Insurance, Municipal and Royal.

• As a matter of local company law the company must maintain a registered office address within Samoa and must also appoint a Samoan resident secretary and registered agent.

2. Samoa Creditor Controlled International Company:

Samoa offers a company without share capital. It is "owned" by the holder(s) of bearer debentures. It is possible to allot a non-voting redeemable preference share to a non-resident of Australia to ensure the company is in fact a "company" rather than some exotic derivative if this is felt necessary.

From 1 July 1990, Australian residents with an interest in a Controlled Foreign Corporation ("CFC") are subject to accruals taxation on the share of the income of the CFC to which they are entitled to receive by virtue of their shareholding unless the CFC is subject to income tax in a comparable tax jurisdiction.

A foreign company's status as a CFC requires it to be controlled by Australian residents. The word "controlled" is not specifically defined in the Income Tax Assessment Act 1936 ("the Act"). There is an argument that control can only vest with shareholders, in which case a Western Samoa Creditor Controlled International Company ("CCIC") whose sole shareholder is not a resident of Australia, but whose Australian investors merely hold bearer debentures, is not a CFC. If this view is correct then none of the provisions of Part X apply to an Australian resident debenture holder and no attribution of income occurs. There are no reporting requirements as the debenture holder is not an attributable taxpayer.

The alternative view is that the subjective de facto control test of section 340(c) of The Act does not require control to vest in shareholders and a CCIC whose fate vests in the hands of an Australian resident debenture holder is a CFC within the meaning of Part X.

Assuming this second view is correct, to enable the Australian resident to be subject to accrual taxation his Attributable Income must be calculated and this is where the provisions of Part X of the Act are seriously deficient. In normal situations an Australian resident's attributable interest in a CFC is the same as his Direct Control Interest under section 356. Where however the subjective de facto control test applies under section 340(c) the resident is deemed, pursuant to section 350(c), to have a direct control interest of 100%, but his Attribution Percentage is calculated in accordance with his actual interest in the CFC as established under section 356(1). This section specifically limits attribution interests to shareholders and share capital.

So under the second view, all of the provisions of Part X of the Act apply to CCIC except the final step. There is no attribution interest held by the Australian resident in the CFC and therefore no attribution is possible. Part X of the Act is aborted and no accruals taxation applies.

Whichever view of the subjective de facto control test of section 340(c) of the Act is correct, attribution of income cannot apply to the Australian resident debenture holder making the CCIC an effective tax deferment entity.

A Samoan Creditor Controlled International Company has the following characteristics:

- CCIC pay no taxes in Samoa.
- As described above a CCIC can operate without share capital and without shareholders and all the usual rights, which would normally be exercised by the shareholders, accrue to the holder of the bearer debenture.
- A minimum of one director is required and corporate directors are permitted. Details do not appear on the public file.
- A brief annual return must be filed but no accounts need be filed. It should be noted that penalties would be incurred if the license fee is not paid when due.
- Names must end with one of the following words, or abbreviations thereof - Limited, Corporation, Incorporated, Societe Anonyme or Sociedad Anonima. The following words, and their associated

activities, cannot be used: Assurance, Bank, Building Society, Chamber of Commerce, Chartered, Cooperative, Imperial, Insurance, Municipal and Royal.

- As a matter of local company law the company must maintain a registered office address within Samoa and must also appoint a Samoan resident as secretary and registered agent.

6.31. Seychelles

The Seychelles is a group of 115 small islands located at the center of the Indian Ocean to the north of Madagascar off the African coast. They were uninhabited until the 17th century and have since been occupied by both the French and the British. They were granted independence from Britain in 1976 and have continued to enjoy major economic, social and political developments. They are now a presidential republic, which forms part of the Commonwealth. The population of 73,000 is a multi-lingual mixture of African, Indian, Chinese and European, although English is the official language. The majority of the population lives on the main island of Mahe. The mainstay of the economy is tourism, although fishing and the development of the jurisdiction as an international business center contribute. In 1993 a new constitution was drafted and the Government of the day implemented legislation designed to turn the country into an international business center. Legislation covered the registration of international business companies and international trusts as well as establishing an international trade zone.

International Companies:

The International Business Company's Acts 1994 was enacted to provide a comprehensive regime for the incorporation, regulation, operation and taxation of International Business Companies. This piece of legislation is extremely flexible and provides for a minimum of disclosure. Meetings need not take place in the Seychelles, and there is no necessity to report changes in shareholders, directors and mortgages to the Registrar.

International Business Companies have the following characteristics:

- International Business Companies are not subject to taxation within the Seychelles.
- An International Business Company needs only one shareholder and shares can be issued in bearer or registered form. Details of the shareholders do not appear on the public file, although a Register of Members must be maintained.
- A minimum of one director is required and corporate directors are permitted. Details of the directors do not appear on the public file, although a Register of Directors must be maintained.
- International Business Companies are not required to file either an annual return or accounts.
- The following words cannot be used: Assurance, Bank, Building Society, Chamber of Commerce, Chartered, Co-operative, Foundation, Government, Imperial, Insurance, Municipal and Trust, or any other words which suggest the patronage of any Government. All company names must end with Limited, Corporation, Incorporated, Societé Anonyme or a similar recognized alternative.
- As a matter of local company law the company must maintain a registered office address within the Seychelles and must also appoint a Seychelles resident as a registered agent
- There are no specific statutory provisions governing secrecy in relation to companies but English Law.

6.32. Singapore

The Republic of Singapore is a British Commonwealth country located at the tip of the Malaysian peninsula and occupying an area of 622 square kilometers. Singapore gained independence from Britain in

1965 but because of its close connection to the Crown the business language is English and the English common law system applies. Local currency is the Singapore Dollar and there is an excellent professional infrastructure with good legal services. Most of the large accountancy firms have offices in Singapore, as do most of the major international banks. Communications are excellent with state of the art telecommunications equipment and an airport, which serves as a regional hub for over 100 destinations.

A Singapore Company:

A Singapore incorporated company may be deemed resident or non-resident depending on its place of central management and control. Thus, in simple terms, a Singapore company, which has a majority of its directors resident in Singapore, will be deemed resident and those, which have a majority of directors resident outside Singapore, would normally be deemed non-resident. The place of central control and management is the only practical difference between a resident and non-resident Singapore company.

All Singapore companies have the following characteristics:

- The current rate of corporation tax is 26%. A Singapore resident company is only taxed on Singapore source income and foreign income which is remitted to Singapore. A non-resident Singapore company would pay tax only on Singapore source income. Please note that for the company to gain the benefit of the double taxation treaties signed by Singapore it is likely that the company would have to be resident. Treaties have presently been concluded with Australia, Bangladesh, Belgium, Canada, China, Denmark, Finland, France, Germany, India, Indonesia, Israel, Italy, Japan, Korea, Malaysia, The Netherlands, New Zealand, Norway, Philippines, Sri Lanka, Sweden, Switzerland, Taiwan, Thailand, and United Kingdom.

- A minimum of two shareholders is required whose details appear on the public register. Corporate shareholders are permitted. Anonymity can be achieved by the use of nominee shareholders.
- A minimum of two directors is required and full details of these must be filed with the Public Registry. Corporate directors are not permitted. One director must be a resident of Singapore and this director remains responsible for the compliance by the company with the Singapore Companies Act and may continue to be liable for those obligations even after resigning. Additionally, if the company wishes to receive relief under the various tax treaties signed by Singapore it is likely that it would be necessary to demonstrate that the company has a majority of Singapore resident directors in order to establish that the company is resident in Singapore for tax purposes. Corporate directors are not permitted.
- All Singapore companies must prepare full audited accounts and must keep a copy of such accounts at the registered office address. All except exempt private companies (a private company with less than 20 members and in which no corporation has a beneficial interest in its shares) must file accounts on the public register.
- Names, which suggest any connection to the UK head of state, are generally prohibited and certain words, which suggest specialist activity, can only be used when the appropriate licenses have been obtained e.g. bank, insurance company and other specialist financial enterprises.
- As a matter of local company law the company must maintain a registered office address within Singapore and must appoint a Singapore resident as company secretary. Additionally the company must appoint at least one Singapore resident director.

6.33. South Africa

South Africa is a former British colony that changed to self-rule in 1948. Subsequently on 30 April 1994 the newly elected Democratic

Government came into power representing all races of the country. South Africa lies at the southern most tip of the continent of Africa and boasts being the "Hong Kong" into sub Saharan Africa. There is an excellent infrastructure with the most up to date telecommunications, air, road and rail. There are approximately 43 million people living within its borders and due to the recent changes in Government there are exceptional opportunities both politically and financially. South African common law applies and in cases where no guidance can be found in our common law the courts draw from experience from English Law under point and issue and follow the English precedents if justified. There is an excellent range of professional services available as South Africa serves as the major business center for the whole of the Sub Saharan continent. The local currency is South African Rand (ZAR) which is interchangeable with other major currencies of the world. There are Exchange Controls, which govern the flow of funds in and out of South Africa. There is a total prohibition on dealing in foreign exchange except with the permission of and on the conditions set by the Treasury.

The South African Company:

There are two types of Private Limited Liability entities in South Africa, the Close Corporation (CC) and a Private Company (PTY).

The Private Company has the following characteristics:

- The rate of Private-Company-Taxation is 35% on South African source income only.
- A minimum of one shareholder is required whose details are filed on the public register. Corporate shareholders are permitted and anonymity can be achieved by the use of nominee shareholders. Membership is limited to a maximum of 50 shareholders.
- A minimum of one director is required and full details of these must be filed with the Public Registry. An annual general meeting must be held within 18 months after the companies incorporation.

Subsequent annual general meetings are to be held not later than 9 months after the end of each ensuing accounting date (the end of the Financial Year) but still within 15 months of the date of the preceding annual general meeting.

- South African companies are required to file full audited accounts and must also prepare and file an annual return which gives details of the current directors and of the shareholders who have held shares in the company at any time during the year.
- There are restrictions on the use of certain words in the name of a company. Specific permission has to be obtained prior to incorporating the company. Words which are deemed to be 'undesirable' or which are 'calculated to deceive or mislead the public' are prohibited.
- As a matter of local company law the company must maintain a registered office address within the jurisdiction of incorporation and must also appoint an auditor.

The Close Corporation has the following characteristics:
- A Close Corporation is governed by the Close Corporations Act of 1984. The Close Corporation provides a simpler and less expensive corporate form for the single entrepreneur or a few participants (who must be natural persons). The name of a Close Corporation ends with the words "Close Corporation" or "CC".
- The CC is a juristic person distinct from its members; it consequently enjoys perpetual succession and its members have limited liability in respect of the Corporations debts.
- The rate of taxation is 35% on South African source income only.
- There are no shareholders. Instead there are members who have a percentage interest in the entity. There is a minimum of one member and a maximum of ten. Companies cannot be members of a CC. There is no register of members however, details of the members are found in the Founding Statement.

- There are no directors. Instead there are members who are in a similar position to directors of a company i.e. members have certain fiduciary duties towards the Corporation. There is a minimum of one member and a maximum of ten. Companies cannot be members of a CC. There is no register of members however, details of the members are found in the Founding Statement.
- There is no requirement to file audited accounts, however, annual financial statements must be prepared by the Corporations "accounting officer" who need not be a qualified Chartered Accountant.
- There are restrictions on the use of certain words in the name of a company. Specific permission has to be obtained prior to incorporating the company. Words which are deemed to be 'undesirable' or which are 'calculated to deceive or mislead the public' are prohibited.
- As a matter of local company law the company must maintain a registered office address within the jurisdiction of incorporation and must also appoint an accounting officer.

6.34. Turks And Caicos Islands

The Turks and Caicos Islands ("TCI") lie 575 miles south east of Miami, with the Bahamas some 30 miles to the northwest. There are 8 principal inhabited islands, which have an estimated population of 13,000. the seat of government and capital is Grand Turk. The legal system is based upon English Common Law with local modifications and the Islands are governed by an Executive Council of ministers appointed from the Legislative Council of elected members presided over by a British appointed Governor. The Islands are a British Crown Colony and Britain maintains responsibility for defense and foreign affairs.

The Turks And Caicos Islands Exempt Company:
One of the foundations upon which the TCI' s success as an offshore center has been built is the Companies Ordinance 1981. This legislation

was closely modeled on the equivalent Cayman Islands law and is extremely flexible and provides in the shape of an exempted company for a minimum of disclosure. Meetings need not take place in the Islands, the objects may be unrestricted and details of shareholders and directors need not appear on any public record. An exempt TCI company receives a certificate issued in the name of the Governor which guarantees that the company will be exempt from all forms of taxation, both in respect of its own operations and on the shares in the company, for a period of 20 years from its date of incorporation. Companies may be incorporated with a translation of the English name appearing on the Certificate of Incorporation. The name may be represented in any foreign language or characters. Additionally, a foreign language translation of the Memorandum and Articles of Association may be officially registered alongside the English version. Thus, for example, the Certificate of Incorporation could bear both an English name and a translation of that name in Chinese characters. A Chinese character version of the Memorandum and Articles of Association could also be registered.

- The TCI are a major no tax haven. There are no direct taxes such as income tax, corporation tax, capital gains tax, profit tax, gift tax or death duties.
- An exempted company need only have one shareholder and shares can be issued in bearer or registered form. There is no requirement to file the details of shareholders on any public record.
- A minimum of one director is required and corporate directors are permitted. There is no requirement to file the details of directors on any public record.
- There is no requirement to file accounts or a detailed annual return. Each company must file a short statement indicating that it has traded mainly outside the islands and that the company has complied with various statutory requirements.

- The following words cannot be used either in English or any other language: Assurance, Bank, Building Society, Commonwealth, Co-operative Society, Fidelity, Friendly Society, Guarantee, Indemnity, Insurance, Re-insurance, Trust, Trustee, Underwriter, Royal, Imperial, Empire, Municipal and Chartered or any derivatives of any of those words without the written consent of the Financial Secretary. The name of an exempt company need not indicate that the company is limited.
- As a matter of local company law the company must maintain a registered office address within the TCI and must also appoint a TCI resident as registered agent.
- Both the Companies Ordinance and the Confidential Relationships Ordinance 1979 make it an offence punishable by a maximum fine of US$ 50,000 and/or a prison sentence of up to 3 years for anybody to reveal confidential information, including details of the owners and directors, about a TCI exempt company or to threaten to reveal such information.

6.35. United Kingdom

The United Kingdom ("U.K.") comprises England, Scotland, Northern Ireland and Wales and is one of the fifteen member states of the European Union. It has an area of some 244,100 square kilometers (94,250 sq. miles) with an estimated population in excess of 57 million. London is one of the world's leading centers for banking, insurance and other financial services; lying between New York and Tokyo it is the third leg of the world's capital markets. Not the least of its attractions is that it is a politically stable English speaking country. The U.K. is strategically located off the Northwest coast of Continental Europe and has excellent communications; it has three major international airports in Heathrow, Gatwick and Manchester with extensive worldwide connections. Recently the U.K. was physically joined to the mainland Continent by the opening of the Channel rail tunnel link, which boasts frequent train services for passengers and cars to Paris and Brussels. The U.K. has signed double taxation treaties with 100 countries and thus enjoys the most extensive double taxation treaty network in the world.

The U.K. Company:

For the purposes of this information sheet an U.K. company is incorporated in England or Wales and registered in Cardiff, Wales. Details on incorporating in Edinburgh, Scotland or Belfast, Northern Ireland are also available.

The U.K. Company has the following characteristics:

• The corporation tax rates are the lowest in the European Union. Tax is levied at 20% on an U.K. company, which has net profits under £300,000. For profits between £300,000 and £1.5 million there will be an effective marginal rate of 32.5% and a tax rate of 30% is levied where the profits are over this figure. Generally speaking, an U.K. company is taxable on its worldwide income at the rates indicated above. However, a U.K. incorporated company may still be classified as non-resident for tax purposes, and therefore non taxable in the U.K. on non U.K. source income, if it is managed and controlled from a country with which the U.K. has signed a double taxation treaty which contains a recognized "tie-breaker clause". By careful selection of the country from which the U.K. Company is managed it may therefore be possible to create a non-taxable U.K. entity. For example, Portugal has a suitable tax treaty with the U.K. so an U.K. company managed from Madeira (Madeira being part of Portugal) would neither be taxable in Madeira nor the U.K. It is important to note that such a U.K. company would not qualify to receive benefits under the tax treaty signed by the U.K. but might qualify for Portuguese tax treaty benefits so the major benefit of this structure is to create a non-taxable entity which has the added respectability of a U.K. persona. Another recent innovation Section 246S of The Taxes Act 1988 (as inserted by Schedule 16 of The Finance Act 1994) creates the U.K. International Headquarters Company ("IHC"). This status may be accorded to ordinary U.K. companies, which are at least 80% beneficially, owned by non-residents. An IHC is an extremely useful vehicle for the collection of foreign dividend income as, in general terms, a full credit is given against U.K. tax for any tax paid on the remitted profits before arrival in the U.K. Thus as long as the dividend income has already suffered tax at a rate higher than or equal to the applicable UK rate (32.5%/30%/20%) no U.K. tax will be payable on that income either on arrival or on distribution. For example, a Danish subsidiary of an U.K. IHC would pay tax on its profits at 34%. If the Danish subsidiary distributed profit by way of dividend to the IHC parent no further tax would be levied on arrival in the U.K. because a credit would be given for tax paid in Denmark. This makes the U.K. IHC an extremely attractive holding company vehicle for investment into Europe or otherwise and in most cases will be more attractive than competitive structures available through the Netherlands, Austria, Switzerland etc.

- An U.K. company must have a minimum of one shareholder who may be a corporate body or an individual. Details of the shareholders appear on public record but anonymity may be retained by the use of nominee shareholders or holding companies.

- An U.K. company must have at least one director and a company secretary. A sole director cannot also be the secretary. The Director can be an individual or a company. If there is more than one director, one of them can also be the secretary but, as U.K. Company law is complex, it is strongly recommended that a professional secretary with relevant experience be appointed. Details of the directors appear on the public file but anonymity can be retained by the use of third party professionals.

- Generally an U.K. company must appoint an auditor and audited accounts must be filed with the Companies Registry within 9 months of the financial year-end. In a large number of cases companies with sales of under £90,000 are exempt from this requirement and those with turnover of less than £350,000 need only produce abbreviated accounts with a special accountants report. An annual return giving details of directors and shareholders is required for all companies.

- The Registrar has the power to refuse registration of any name, which he considers undesirable or too similar to an existing company. A name will not be allowed if it is misleading - for example, if it suggests that a company with small resources is trading on a great scale or over a wide field. Names cannot ordinarily be allowed if they suggest connection with the Crown or Government Departments.
- As a matter of local company law the company must maintain a registered office address within the U.K. and must also appoint a company secretary who, for practical reasons, must be resident in the U.K.
- There are no specific laws relating to the unauthorized disclosure of information on an U.K. company, its directors or owners.

6.36. Vanuatu

Vanuatu, located 1,500 miles northeast of Australia, became independent in 1980. Vanuatu has a political and legal system that closely follows the UK being a parliamentary democracy based on the Westminster system, and the law is based on English law. The official languages are French and English, and the currency is the "Vatu". The 80 small islands that make up Vanuatu are administered from Port Vila, and are connected to the outside world by excellent telecommunications and flights to major cities in Australia and New Zealand. The International Companies Act passed in December 1992 provides for the incorporation of the International Company (IC) which is preferred over the exempt company. IC's do not have the concept of authorized capital.

The Vanuatu IC:

- ICs pay no taxes in Vanuatu. Upon incorporation ICs are exempt from taxes for 20 years.
- A minimum of one director is required and corporate directors are permitted. Details of the directors do not appear on the public file.
- No annual return or accounts need be filed. The company does not have to hold annual general meetings. If the company fails to pay the Government tax on or before 30 June of each year, the tax will be increased by 10% every month that it remains unpaid up to 50%.
- Names must end with one of the following words, or abbreviations thereof - Limited, Corporation, Incorporation, Sendirian Berhad, Besloten Vennootschap, Gesellschaft mit beschrankter Haftung. Names will not be allowed that in are, the opinion of the Registrar, likely to mislead or deceive, or suggest a connection with the Government of Vanuatu.
- As a matter of local company law the company must maintain a registered office address within Vanuatu and must also appoint a Vanuatu resident as registered agent.
- The International Companies Act makes it a criminal offence for any person to divulge information concerning an IC.

About the Author

Levent Gülkök is Executive Vice President of Samuel Goldberg Consulting, an international network of companies. Born in Turkey, he immigrated with his parents to Germany where he studied Economics. Serving management positions in investment sector, he changed to the business and finance sector. Today, with his wife and his son, he is living in Paris and manages business throughout the world.

www.ingramcontent.com/pod-product-compliance
Lightning Source LLC
Chambersburg PA
CBHW030816180526
45163CB00003B/1303